Ulrike Bronner, Clarissa Reikersdorfer
Urban Nomads Building Shanghai

Urban Studies

Ulrike Bronner (Dipl.-Ing.) is working in an interdisciplinary team offering strategic consultancy services for construction projects. Her focus lies on the communication between project stakeholders.
Clarissa Reikersdorfer (Dipl.-Ing.) is a Research Fellow at the Chair for Sustainable Spatial Development at the University of Liechtenstein. She works on sustainability issues and responsibility of architects.

Ulrike Bronner, Clarissa Reikersdorfer
Urban Nomads Building Shanghai
Migrant Workers and the Construction Process

[transcript]

With the friendly support of the State of Vorarlberg (Land Vorarlberg).

Bibliographic information published by the Deutsche Nationalbibliothek
The Deutsche Nationalbibliothek lists this publication in the Deutsche Nationalbibliografie; detailed bibliographic data are available in the Internet at http://dnb.d-nb.de

© 2016 transcript Verlag, Bielefeld

All rights reserved. No part of this book may be reprinted or reproduced or utilized in any form or by any electronic, mechanical, or other means, now known or hereafter invented, including photocopying and recording, or in any information storage or retrieval system, without permission in writing from the publisher.

Cover layout: Kordula Röckenhaus, Bielefeld
Printed and bound in Great Britain by Marston Book Services Ltd, Oxfordshire
Print-ISBN 978-3-8376-3344-3
PDF-ISBN 978-3-8394-3344-7

Table of Content

Preface | 7
Introduction | 11

1. Interacting with Urban China | 19
1.1 Contemporary Critical Urban Studies | 19
1.2 China's Rapid Urbanization | 23
1.3 Construction – A Process | 26
1.4 Participants – Who is Involved? | 27

2. People in Motion | 31
2.1 Labour Migration | 33
2.2 Labour Migration in China | 35
2.3 The International Business Migrant | 40
2.4 A Peculiarity: the Similarities | 41

3. Urban Nomads – Permanently Temporary | 45
3.1 Emerging Challenges in Migration Studies | 48
3.2 Tailor-Made City Planning and Cocooned Living | 49

4. Shanghai – Head of the Concrete Dragon | 55
4.1 Urban Transformation in Shanghai | 56
4.2 Impacts on the Lived Space | 58
4.3 Construction Sites as Research Field | 60

5. Global Urban Nomads | 63
5.1 Approaching from Within | 63
5.2 The Wide Field of Expatriates | 64
5.3 Bubble Worlds – Spatial Conditions | 70
5.4 Working Challenges | 73

6. Rural Urban Nomads | 81
6.1 Approaching from Outside | 82
6.2 Working Conditions on Site | 83
6.3 Spatial Configurations | 89
6.4 Social Situation | 93

7. Reflecting on Urban Nomads | 101
7.1 Reflecting on Global Urban Nomads | 102
7.2 Reflecting on Rural Urban Nomads | 104
7.3 Interrelations between Urban Nomads | 105
7.4 Urban Nomads' Right to Shanghai | 108

8. Prospects | 111
8.1 Fair Building | 111
8.2 From Idea to Action | 115

Acknowledgement | 119
Glossary | 121
Bibliography | 123
Table of Figures | 135

Preface

BY SABINE KNIERBEIN

Paths of urban development and architectural construction in China have been thought of as a product of a Chinese state in radical transition towards a capitalist marked regime. This observation is connected with insights on the new emergence of special economic zones and a new round of up-scaled and up-speeded capitalist restructuring never witnessed in the Western world at such a scale and scope. Western Architecture Offices have popped up and the Chinese formal bureaucratic system is facing the opening of an increasing number of Western businesses in their territory. While much of the focus on Chinese urbanism has been set on lighthouse architects and their contributions to shaping the palimpsest of newly invented old cities and urban patterns, contributions that tackle the working and living conditions related to the places of construction are hard to find both in China and in the Western world. In this book, Ulrike Bronner and Clarissa Reikersdorfer address this gap with due diligence – an ethnography and creative critique of these conditions of architectural projects and construction sites. Besides sociological accounts on the urban code in Asia that promote an ideal-type understanding of the new Chinese city, the authors of this book have developed their contribution out of extensive empirical fieldwork on construction sites in Shanghai. This publication is not only the result of what they have observed and encountered, but it also offers insights into the challenging world of researchers' feelings torn between the charming meetings of Western expat architects in embassies and diplomatic climate, and the face-to-face encounters with regional construction workers without a legal status – which resemble both the current labour force and the new reserve army in the Chinese capitalist urban production circuit.

Puzzled by the striking discrepancies between international business migration of architects to China who tend to live in "spatial cocoons", and those workers living partly with their families on the very same construction sites, Clarissa Reikersdorfer and Ulrike Bronner reveal a phenomenon that affects around one-third of Shanghai's current population: a nomadic way of life to make their living to build Shanghai. It is exactly this unbearable discrepancy that became the authors' main drive for the surpassing code of professional ethics, the above-average analytical skills and the outstanding critical position. Both Ulrike Bronner and Clarissa Reikersdorfer brought along remarkable competences which were further developed during their research in China.

Reading their final book resembles a firework of insights because firstly, both authors have been able to expand their initially city-based work to a consideration of global urbanization processes in China, a country that, according to the Chinese Statistical Yearbook from 2014, currently hosts over 253 million internal working migrants. Secondly, the two architects have developed a mobile educational architecture called *Yidong Ketang* – a pop-up training shelter structure for construction workers in Shanghai – for which they have been awarded the Social Impact Award in Vienna in 2011. Thirdly, the young scientists have engaged into debates about fair building, that is, the necessary integration of human rights perspectives (e.g. decent living and working conditions) into the current codes of ethics of international architects working in China (and elsewhere). Finally, the book is a contribution that triggers a debate about social sustainability certificates for construction processes to reconnect producers and consumers of global architecture between cities and continents.

Above all, their work shows the relevance of and need for critical urban research based on the everyday life of people involved in construction processes, which largely remain unconsidered by our own professions. By theoretically reframing the construction site as a social process, Ulrike Bronner and Clarissa Reikersdorfer have produced an outstanding work of the highest relevance for architects and planners in China. They have also taught a lesson for the revision of future academic curricula as regards the integration of human needs and rights into an education that "produces" internationally working urban professionals.

The status of temporary working migrants in Chinese construction processes make the two very distinct groups that have been tackled during this research – the regional workers and the international architects – share one basic feature in common: They both share the new permanence of global and regional temporary migration and the ways they live in the cities on an everyday basis which is restricted to spatial cocoons, with hardly any access to public spaces and an integration into the formal Chinese urban society. Critical research on the growing precarity and fragmentation of the globalized city is analysed as if magnified under a burning glass: The social processes on architectural construction sites are a key entry window to understand current phenomena of the social production of urban space.

The book is a must-have for socially concerned architects, teachers in planning, architecture and urban studies who are interested in a constructive, yet critical dialogue between Asia and Europe, but also beyond. It sheds light on the precarious living conditions of construction workers around the world. It connects the architect not just to the finally produced architecture, but to the architectural production process in conditions of global urbanization. It helps those interested in becoming urban researchers to find a way to define their own positionality in times of seemingly post-political urban planning and urban design regimes.

"Urban Nomads. Building Shanghai. Migrant Workers and the Construction Process" by Ulrike Bronner and Clarissa Reikersdorfer includes stunning empirical field work and parts of a warm-hearted research diary. It has been awarded the Arch Diploma Price for Best Theoretical Thesis at the Faculty of Architecture and Planning at Technische Universität Wien in Austria in 2011/2012. The book is a fearless and courageous essential for architecture as a discipline that ideally defines ethical standards of globalized work in their (national) code of ethics and asks for an urgent revision of teaching curricula in the same field to prepare their future graduates for a growingly globalized labour market. It asks for the need to reconnect architectural production to decent working standards and deplores the systematic failure to comply with minimum working and living standards on globalized construction sites.

Ass. Prof. Dr. Sabine Knierbein leads the Interdisciplinary Centre for Urban Culture and Public Space at the Faculty of Architecture and Planning at the Technische Universität Wien in Austria.

Introduction

This is not an analysis, nor is it a narration or description of events that breaks down the Chinese urbanization process into small details. In many ways urban phenomena are too complex, too big, and too fast to be fully understood or to be made explainable by breaking them down into comprehensible elements. The development of megacities is a global phenomenon that is particularly visible in contemporary China. In no other country is the process of urbanization occurring at such a large scale and with such speed. Urban transformation is taking place at a pace that has not been seen before and we as observers can only try breathlessly to keep up. Mostly, we follow the results and evaluate them after they have happened rather than while they are occurring. Fascinated by this rapid urbanization, we came to Beijing and Shanghai to study and work for several times between 2008 and 2015. During our working experience in the field of architecture we repeatedly witnessed things that appeared puzzling within the construction process and the question *"weishenme?"* 为什么 – why? – constantly aroused our curiosity. When visiting construction sites we were unpleasantly surprised to see laundry hanging in half demolished houses and building shells. Why do Chinese construction workers live on the construction site? Why are so many architects moving to Shanghai? Why are so many poor-quality buildings erected so quickly? *Weishenme* – 为什么.

This book is a collection of snapshots, of close-ups of urban transformation – but it is not about the city itself as an object of study, but rather is about the countless people who make this transformation possible. What makes them move to the city? And what does it mean for them to be in a new environment far away from family and friends? This is about their circumstances and capabilities, their personal motives and their dreams.

Figure 1: Laundry Hanging in a Half Demolished House in Shanghai

Source. Bronner | Reikersdorfer 2008

"We don't pay enough tribute to the backbone of Shanghai's construction fervor, as unhappy as Shanghai residents seem to be by all the Expo-driven noise and air pollution. We crane our necks to identify the peaks of skyscrapers that overrun the city but tend to sweep over the ubiquitous orange and red helmets dotting the sides of streets – hauling concrete, climbing into sewers and soldering windows in unfinished buildings. They are migrant labor that are building the China dream but are rarely able to enjoy the luxurious fruits which the well-off take for granted. They are also the unrecognized residents of Shanghai, and in many cases, looked down upon because they are mostly from out of the city, or 外地人 (*wai di ren*) from poorer and far-flung provinces of China. Perhaps they make enough to help the family back home to buy a pig or send their children to school. If they are lucky, they can help their families buy a television with the help of generous rural subsidies that the government recently introduced.

This gentleman, in a group of mingling workers, was most pleased to have his portrait taken in front of the Shanghai World Financial Centre (SWFC) as his workplace backdrop. Upon looking at the resulting image, he scratched his head and stared back at the building, as if it had never occurred to him to do so. For having poured their blood, sweat and tears into building Shanghai's skyline for minimum wage, they ultimately have no ownership or belonging in that part of China's dream." (Sue Anne Tay 2009: The face of Shanghai's skyline)

Figure 2: Builders of Shanghai's Skyline

Source. Bronner I Reikersdorfer 2014

"In Shanghai today, opportunity seems to vibrate on the streets. It reads on people's faces as they go about their business or walk the river embankment and the commercial sidewalks. And part of the opportunity – and the fun – lies in the city's enormous diversity. In 2003, Robert Venturi and I were invited to China to lecture and consult on campus planning and architecture. We accepted the invitation in order to see the country and to work as architects, but also to indulge our fascination with China's culture and with its centuries of cultural interaction, worldwide.
[...]
And I fantasized about coming to Shanghai on a voyage of discovery – in search of new urban prototypes and spending a working vacation in the city, in a spa hotel attached to a scholar's garden. Every morning, after my sauna, I would follow the way of the ancient scholar, down his paths, up his little hill, to his small summer house with a long view, and set myself up in there and do my work." (Denise Scott Brown in Gil 2008: 71-87)

As different as these two perspectives on Shanghai might be, they both describe phenomena of the construction process. Both are part of a complex system of urbanization and part of the Chinese construction boom, which in addition to its speed and dynamics is also thrilling and exciting for various other reasons. But while the mushrooming high-rises are being celebrated as still-life art work through representative architectural photography in glossy magazines on modern city life, the process of planning and erecting the buildings is relegated to the background. The whole system of construction that lies behind this production of space is not visible and the role of the architect as planner in this turbo-urbanism as well as the magnitude of the task taken on by the executing parties is not given sufficient attention.

Proceeding from pure curiosity about the puzzles of city development and urban transformation we soon found that certain supposedly universally recognized principles of equality and self-determination of people are missing from the construction business. As early as 1996, UN Habitat declared that "urban poverty and its attendant human cost is perhaps the single greatest challenge of our time" (UN Habitat 1996). On a global level cities have become increasingly homogenous and have grown together, but internally they are more and more divided by increasing inequality and spatial fragmentation. By focusing on the building process and construction sites we want to look behind the scenes and illuminate the "backstage activities" that are part of shiny, large-scale projects. In various snapshots of the spatial and social DNA of Shanghai we aim to show the links between the physical and the social in cities.

This book is an examination of a very specific group of people: individuals who are involved in various construction processes over time. The ongoing building boom in China has caused them to follow their work without settling permanently due to the temporary nature of building projects. Among the people involved in the construction process in China, two groups must be emphasized – because they include such a large number of people that it is important to investigate their role in the construction process. But there are several additional reasons to pay close attention to these groups – torn away from their homes, they have many things in common while remaining completely different. And while their existence is recognized by the media, scholarly research has not paid them sufficient attention.

This work is based on research conducted between 2008 and 2015 in Shanghai; inter alia supported by the Technical University of Vienna and Tongji University. The goal of this participatory observation was to examine flows of working migrants in Shanghai's building and construction processes. The main task of the on-site investigation was visiting various construction sites in and around

Shanghai and observing the workings of several private planning offices and gain direct insights from migrant workers.

What is happening in Chinese cities today is of historic importance. However, finding a language that does justice to the city's social, economic, and political landscape is challenging. Our study begins on various different but interrelated levels and attempts to grasp the complexity of the current urban transformations going on in China.

The first part of the book, Interacting With Urban China, begins with a discussion of our understanding of city development and urban planning. Besides the familiar debate on the quality of buildings erected at such enormous speed in Chinese cities, it is often forgotten that construction is more than the materialized final result. In the language of critical urban studies, space is neither just a materialized end result nor a pure concept, but rather is a social process of production. The chapter on the Production Of Space is mainly based on Lefebvre's theories when describing the relationships between the production of the built environment and societal processes.

The following chapter, Construction – A Process, focuses on construction phases as described in the disciplines of project management and project development by highlighting the relationships and dependencies that are part of the construction process. From the beginning of a project until the building is actually used and reused, many different groups with various professional and even cultural backgrounds are involved. We refer to the minimum standards of human rights according to the UN and the International Labour Organization (ILO) and use this as a benchmark for all actors involved.

After introducing the broad range of actors involved in building projects, we refer to the assumption that migrant workers play a specific role in construction processes in China in general and in Shanghai in particular. In the chapter People In Motion we demonstrate how mobile migrant workers strongly affect China's development and how rural-to-urban migration is rapidly reshaping the spatial, economic, demographic, and social landscapes of the Chinese city and countryside. Giving a historical overview of migration in China during Mao Zedong's regime and during the post-Mao period enables us to consider the new phase of urbanization in contemporary China in a historical context. These observations are complemented by our analysis of another group of migrants, for whom the key driver of migration is also employment: International business migrants. Even though the circumstances surrounding these two migration flows are completely different, they do share various characteristics.

Much of the chapter Urban Nomads details our goal of helping to shift the perception of the migrant workers from passive, victimized migrants to active participants in urban life. Similar to traditional nomads, the two groups usually lead a temporary existence over a long period of time and instead of losing their identity by virtue of this migrancy they should be empowered to strengthen their potential within the urban realm. Rural migrant workers and international business migrants who are temporarily involved in construction processes in China are participants in city life. While they actively shape the city through the projects they are working on, they are also individuals living in the city. The naming of the observed groups as urban nomads thus clarifies their special role as permanently temporary individuals as opposed to a mere analysis of the involved migrant workers. The chapter closes with the core arguments for our further investigation on three different levels, as described in three hypotheses.

In Shanghai – Head Of The Concrete Dragon we introduce our approach to our two case studies on international and internal working migrants as an integrative interpretation of urban transformations over time. Shanghai is a global city with over 23 million inhabitants, of whom around 40 percent are a floating population without proper registration, a city that is constantly negotiating what it means to be modern and what it means to be Chinese. The transformation of urban space is manifested not only in a flood of new construction, but also in the changing urban culture and lifestyles of residents. When looking closely at the objects of our research – construction sites in and around Shanghai – some special features become apparent. Construction sites are situated in the setting of existing urban development, dominating the changing urban landscape and at the same time contributing to the rapid transformation of these spaces. Like the transitory people we are observing, the place itself is impermanent and undergoing constant change.

In our first case study we describe what this means in detail for the sphere of global urban nomads, where we, as international business migrants, were also part of the observed group. We highlight the dynamics of urban change in Shanghai under foreign influence, which includes service packages provided by support companies and various networks of belonging in the form of clubs, associations, and internet communities especially for expatriates. Further observations relate to the spatial conditions of international business migrants in Shanghai. Originally restricted to living in hotel-style apartments in approved areas, the international community has now exerted a strong influence upon the real estate market. When we shift our attention to the challenges of working, it becomes clear that working in China is difficult in many ways, but it also offers nearly infinite opportunities for Western professional planners.

In a second case study with a slightly different research approach, we focus on the circumstances of rural migrant construction workers. In the chapter Rural

Urban Nomads we first analyse working conditions, including the structure of working relationships on site, demographic characteristics of workers such as level of education and age, and difficulties they encounter relating to job security, working hours, wage levels, and insurance. Based on several construction site visits we have further observed the spatial configurations of migrant workers and present a detailed breakdown of housing conditions, which are usually less than desirable with prefabricated dormitories situated directly on the construction site. Our analysis finds that the typical patterns of family life are quite scattered and that individual freedom is extremely limited as a result of working and living on site. The final section contextualises for our observations by describing the social, political and legal situation that influences the lives of rural migrant workers in the city. In various debates the social status within the Chinese society is defined through the registration system (*hukou*).

After an interpretation of our findings, we reflect on the techniques used in both case studies. Further, we compare the conclusions of other related research to those made in our study and point out gaps in our research that require further investigation. Finally, we highlight a number of prospects for future action with regard to these socio-spatial transformations. We address several central arguments for a socially just and sustainable form of urbanization by offering possible strategies for future construction. We propose scenarios wherein urban planners, designers, and architects could include fair building processes in their concepts and builders, contractors, and construction managers could support the fair realization of projects. The arguments for *Fair Building* ultimately form the framework for our concluding section – a mobile vocational school for migrant construction workers. This educational programme works toward a solution by addressing all participants in construction to support a building process that goes beyond the traditional audience and contributes to a socially conscious architecture.

1. Interacting with Urban China

1.1 Contemporary Critical Urban Studies

Figure 3: Shanghai Street Life.

Source. Bronner | Reikersdorfer 2011

Everyday Life: Looking through the window of the little kiosk, the *xiaomaibu*, one is confronted with a framed view of a typical scene of Shanghai street life: people passing by on bicycles with huge loads on their bike trailers, school children in their uniforms stopping to buy snacks, motor bikes honking. The street is

particularly vibrant and busy in the morning. People rush by on their way to work while eating their breakfast, while elderly men and women sit all day at the lane's entrance, children play with toys, near the gate guard and the residential committee's leaders.This scene is displayed as a movie inside of the original kiosk where it was shot – now located now inside the ddmwarehouse gallery at the Red Town, Shanghai Sculpture Space.
For the exhibition 'Double Act' 2010 the young Chinese artist Xu Zhifeng aka Shaw worked together with the German artist Petra Johnson to record this spontaneous and authentic Shanghai street culture that is slowly being erased through rapid urbanization. Localized kiosks in Cologne, Liverpool, and Shanghai have been connected with video feeds over the internet, so local residents can communicate across great distances.
The intention is to transform the kiosk from a provider of products for daily use for those in its immediate surroundings into a cultural space connected to the world. The art project gives a small glimpse of recent urban transformations and their environmental effects, as well as China's shift towards the West. The removal of the kiosk also stands as an example of the reckless urban development taking place in China that often doesn't consider local communities. Now this *xiaomaibu* has disappeared from the streets of Shanghai and has been replaced by one of the shiny new large-scale apartment compounds.
(Research Notes, November 2010)

To understand the "dichotomous organization of space and society" and how society organizes itself, a contextualization is needed that includes local specificities as well as globalized patterns (Madanipour 2003: 102). Therefore, in order to lay the groundwork for a basic understanding of the production of social space this chapter provides an overview of some of the key arguments of in contemporary critical urban studies. We aim to employ these concepts as a way of reading between the lines of urban space and adding new perspectives to it.

"Space [...] is unable to provide form, meaning or finality. [...] space is only a medium, environment and means, an instrument and intermediary. [...] It never possesses existence 'in itself' but always refers to something else, to existential and simultaneously essential time, subjective and objective, fact and value, because it is a supreme 'good' for the living, whether they well or badly, because it is simultaneously end and means." (Lefebvre 2003 [1970]: 73)

In the familiar debate about the quality of contemporary Chinese buildings that are erected at such speed, it is often forgotten that construction is more than the materialized end result. Following arguments from critical urban studies, space is not just a (material) object, nor is it a pure idea; it is also a societal process of production (ibid.) It is crucial to understand production of space as a social phenomenon. Thus the main focus of our analysis within the study lies in the relationships between the production of the built environment and the people who are involved in the construction process.

Lefebvre's theory considers the concept of everyday life and demands meaningful lives for all (Shield 1999). Furthermore, he highlights the importance of contextualizing the ongoing practice in relation to space and place; this means it is an issue for planning theory as well as for practice and implementation (Graham/Healey 1999). As a result the shape of the city and the characteristics of urban life are strongly influenced by their social organization. We emphasize the necessity of taking them into account as a part of prospective planning approaches. "For Lefebvre [...] social space is simultaneously a means of production as land and social forces of production as space. As real estate property, spatial relations can be considered part of the social relations of production (the economic base)". In addition, "space is an object of consumption, a political instrument, and an element of social struggle" (Shield 1999: 160).

Figure 4: Three Components of the Social Production of Space

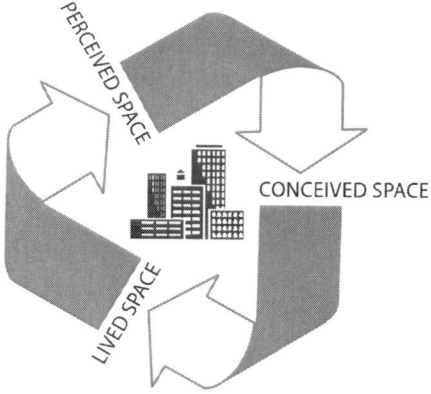

Source. Illustration Bronner I Reikersdorfer, based on Lefebvre 2003 [1970]

Box 1: Three Components of the Social Production of Space

- Perceived space
"Spatial practice with all its contradictions in everyday life, space perceived (percu) in the commonsensical mode – or better still, ignored one minute and over-fetishised the next."
" [...] perception is understood as practical perception [...] and common sense. What remains more important,..., is the notion of taken for granted and unreflective practice." (Shields 1999: 160f)
- Conceived space
"Representation of space,; the discursive regimes of analysis, spatial and planning professions and expert knowledge that conceive of space"
"Representations of space are the logic and forms of knowledge, and the ideological content of codes, theories, and the conceptual depictions of space linked to production relations." (Shields 1999: 161f)
- Lived space
"Space of representation, the third term or other in Lefebvre's three-part dialectic. This is space as it might be, fully lived space, which bursts forth as [...] moments of presence [...]. It is derived from both historical sediments within the everyday environment and from utopian elements that shock one into a new conception of the spatialization of social life." (Shields 1999: 161f)

Source. Shields 1999, based on theories of Henri Lefebvre 1974

We are aware that most theories in critical urban studies are written by Western scholars. Therefore, it is imperative to consider different perspectives in the Chinese context. As Hassenpflug (2010:8) argues, it is important to understand "the urban code of China"– including the "language", "grammar", and "syntax," in order to read the structures and patterns of Chinese cities. In this book we contextualize contemporary practices and mechanisms of the production of built space not just on the macro-level of planning authorities, but also on the micro-level of everyday life in China. Indeed, "Our everyday life-world consists of concrete 'phenomena'. It consists of people." (Norberg-Schulz 1980: 116). People, who are planning and building the city they are living in.

1.2 CHINA'S RAPID URBANIZATION

Figure 5: Construction Site near Kunshan/Shanghai.

Source. Bronner | Reikersdorfer 2011

"China is big, diverse, complex and rapidly changing." (McKinsey 2009: 46).

As China moves towards globalization with competitive and unregulated markets and with its open door policy, this form of turbo-capitalism is leading to a "turbo-urbanism" – a spontaneous uncontrolled urbanism, which still needs to find its form of self regulation (Campanella 2008). To understand China's recent transformation it is necessary to acknowledge that the last 30 years of reforms cannot be easily generalized into an all-encompassing theory. Sociologist Kwan Lee calls it "accumulation without disposition" and understands Chinese development as a process on its own terms (Ching Kwan Lee 2011). In general, the worldwide and regional restructuring of cities combined with mechanisms of socioeconomic development represents a newly practiced neoliberal urbanism (Brenner/Peck/Theodore 2009).

Although China is shifting towards this capitalist production of space, reforms depend on the decisions of the Chinese Communist Party (CCP) and are not liberated from state interference, which makes China a unique case (Friedmann 2005). In addition, the so called "Confucian Capitalism", where Confucian ideology, such as acceptance of hierarchy, valuing perseverance and thrift as well as a collectivist outlook are combined with neoliberal practice, is significant in China's ascent (Rutten 2010). However, the capitalistic practice of the "production of space" enters the city planning process and leads toward a profit-driven urbanization with its relentless commodification and re-commodification of urban space (Brenner/Marcuse/Mayer 2009).

Today, Chinese urbanism in general and in Shanghai in particular manifests itself in new commercial centres, central business districts (CBDs), and westernized apartment buildings (Hassenpflug 2010). Chinese cities are "shooting skyward and exploding outward" and this generates its own dilemmas (Hsing You-Tian 2010). Not only economic and political changes but also structural transitions in society make the ongoing urban transformation of China possible. Therefore, cities are not just a reflection of the relation between production and consumption, between supply and demand, but are an ambivalent producer, product, and a production and consumption process at the same time, as Knierbein points out in the context of public space (2010). Along with this a consumer-oriented, pragmatic liberal and urban civil society is emerging with a rising and expanding middle class, which has an enormous need for newly built residential areas (Zhu Jieming 2000). Thus, the current spatial transformation of Chinese cities is happening at a rapid pace and often without consideration for the inhabitants. China's new cityscape is defined by speed, scale, spectacle, sprawl, and segregation (Campanella 2008).

Nowhere else in the world cities are built up as quickly as in China, a country in a "phase of rapid economic development, ranking number 1 in the world terms of annual building volume, with significantly growing consumption of resources year by year" (GB/T 50378 2006: 23). According to the World Bank (2015), in 2014 54 percent of China's population lived in urban areas, compared to 2000 when only 36.1 percent of Chinese lived in cities and towns.

In each case the spatial impact of urbanism is clearly visible and China is "preparing for its urban billion" (McKinsey Global Institute 2009). Based on growth as a continuing economic engine the study by McKinsey estimated that 350 million people will be added to China's urban population by 2025. The intention is to further stimulate economic growth and justify China's growth rate. However, it becomes obvious that urban residents are facing intense competition and are under enormous pressure to cover basic living costs due to the intensification and extension of the urbanization process.

Box 2: The Vision of China's Urbanization in 2025.

- 350 million will be added to China's urban population by 2025 – more than the population of today's United States
- 1 billion people will live in China's cities by 2030
- 221 Chinese cities will have more than one million citizens – Europe has 35 such cities today
- 5 billion square meters of road will be paved
- 170 mass transit systems will be operating
- 40 billion square meters of floor space will be built – in five million buildings
- 50,000 of these buildings could be skyscrapers – the equivalent to constructing up to ten New York cities
- 5 times – the number by which GDP will have multiplied by 2025

Source. McKinsey Global Institute 2009: 6-7

"The urban phenomenon, taken as a whole, cannot be grasped by any specialized science" (Lefebvre 2003 [1970]: 53). In this context Chinese urbanization becomes a question of scale and complexity. To identify problems in their entirety a interdisciplinary approach is crucial in order to understand the urban phenomenon and its many facets. Therefore, we have integrated social, cultural, economic, and political analysis to further connect it with perspectives on micro-, meso- and macro levels of Chinese processes of production and reproduction of space. This includes an analysis of city planning, residential space, architecture, daily life, and cultural history in a cross-disciplinary exploration of the past, the latent possibilities of present developments, and the future. By bringing together the realms of social science, project management analysis driven by economics and architectural aspects, we are adding different layers and different perspectives to gain insight into the Chinese production of built space. The intention is for the reader to gain a variety of perspectives on the complex Chinese urban phenomenon. Our approach relies on contemporary planning theory and debates in social science. It has to be understood as a flexible framework enabling phenomenological research led by openness and multidimensionality (Knierbein 2010: 401).

The rapid on-going urbanization is highly interrelated with a capitalistic driven construction boom and is also influenced by the changing balance of social forces, power relations, socio-spatial inequalities, and political-institutional arrangements (Brenner/Marcuse/Mayer 2009). Thus, before going into detail, we provide a brief introduction of construction as a process.

1.3 Construction – A Process

Construction is a complex process of bringing design into reality with a defined timeline, scopes of action for various disciplines. A variety of different stakeholders with several areas of expertise are required to deliver the contractually agreed-upon results. When considering processes in construction it is important to understand the overall linkages between the involved, their role, their position in the process, and their dependencies. In order to understand the organization of a construction site and sequence of the construction process as our objects of interest, instruments from the disciplines of project management and project development are utilized. This takes into account economic, technical, legal, organizational, and scheduling tasks for the target-driven implementation of construction projects (DVP 2011). The construction industry is a goal oriented business, with focus on the final result and a linear way of thinking (Kochendörfer/-Liebchen/Viering 2008). The principle of project management for successful project realization implies that particular attention needs to be paid to an efficient project organization structure and to the involvement of qualified experts. Thus a building process can be broken down into a concrete timeline beginning with the project idea and concluding with the actual use of the building, based on internationally approved project standards certified by the Project Management Institute (PMI 2011). In order to complete a construction project following key working stages (RIBA 2013) are required:

- Stage 0: Strategic Definition
- Stage 1: Preparation and Brief
- Stage 2: Concept Design
- Stage 3: Developed Design
- Stage 4: Technical Design
- Stage 5: Construction
- Stage 6: Hand Over and Close out
- Stage 7: In Use & Aftercare

Figure 6: Key Stages of the Construction Process

Stage 0	Stage 1	Stage 2	Stage 3	Stage 4	Stage 5	Stage 6	Stage 7
Strategic Definition	Preparation and Brief	Concept Design	Developed Design	Technical Design	Construction	Hand Over and Close Out	In Use

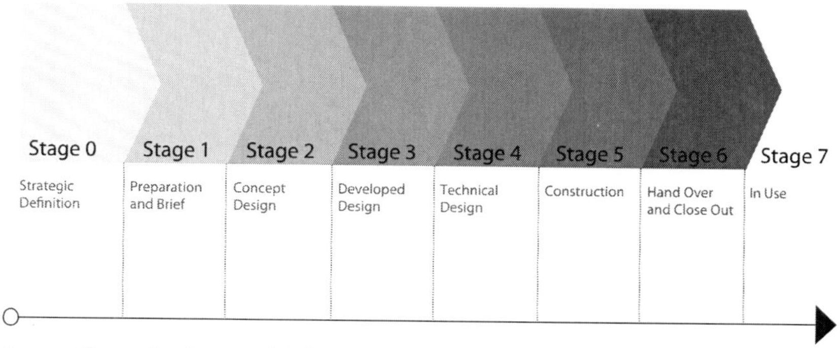

Source. Illustration Bronner | Reikersdorfer based on RIBA Work Stages 2013

1.4 Participants – Who is Involved?

Many different stakeholders with various professional and sometimes even different cultural backgrounds are involved from the starting point of a project until the actual use and reuse of the building. According to project management principles a stakeholder is a person, group or organization, who has a direct or indirect stake in a process. They can affect or be affected by the process action, objectives, and policies (Wiegand 2008). It is therefore of great importance to understand construction as a process with various stakeholders, each of whom pursues their own specific interests within the process. As Figure 7 shows, a typical project management scenario involves various stakeholders within the construction process. Although stakeholding is self-legitimizing, not all stakeholders are equal and different stakeholders have purview over different areas.

Figure 7: Stakeholders. Who is Involved?

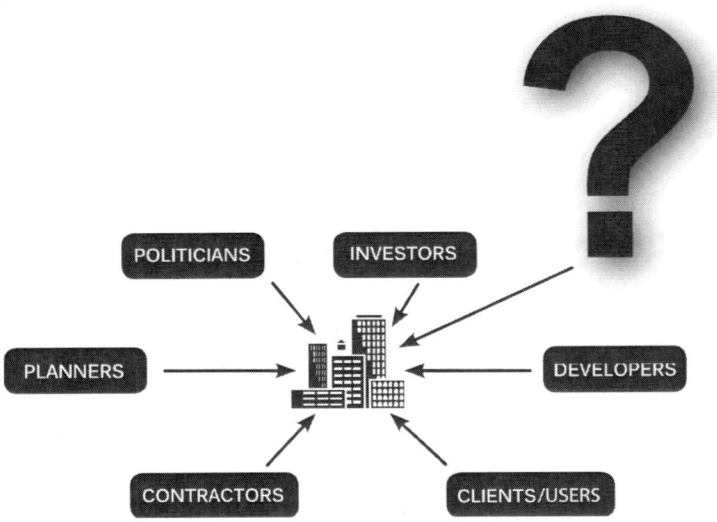

Source. Illustration Bronner | Reikersdorfer 2011

In addition, the term stakeholder implies a certain amount of rights and duties. However, the construction industry often operates according to top down principles, where decisions are made by a small group of people at the expense of a larger group of people, which leads to social injustice during the construction process (Pun Ngai 2010). Based on the unequal power relations that are part of a building process, it seems more accurate to speak not of stakeholders but of participants. We thus place great importance on the observation of the role of rural migrant workers and international business migrants during the process of production as well as their impact on everyday life in Chinese cities, particularly in Shanghai. One of our goals is to recognize that they are an important part of the Chinese construction industry, and to call attention to their needs and demands and give them a stake in the process.

By emphasizing that the production of buildings is a process with the understanding that not every involved person is a stakeholder, we are adding to the ongoing argument that it is not enough to value the success of a project by only considering its materialized end result. In addition to the goal of the building being accepted by its users, the focus should also be on social well-being during the construction process.

In this context it becomes obvious that it is necessary to go beyond current practice – a step towards a more social practice that considers existing legal framework as already stated in the international labour standards monitored by the International Labour Organization (ILO). These standards rely on the Universal Declaration of Human Rights, Articles 23 and 24: "…the ILO helps advance the creation of decent work and the economic and working conditions that give working people and business people a stake in lasting peace, prosperity and progress (ILO 2011)."

In the context of this work, when dealing with marginalization, exclusion, and injustice during the construction process we refer to the need for a profound engagement in the planning phase to achieve greater social and environmental equity by critically examining how space is produced in China. Obviously buildings are erected through the tour de force of construction itself. Therefore, we consider it crucial to have a basic understanding of construction as a process with the different building phases, periods, regulations, and loops. Under which conditions and what terms is construction occurring? And who is involved in this process of the construction of space in China?

2. People in Motion

> "Migration incorporates an understanding of emergent urbanism, process of integration, and everyday social interactions of migrant and established communities, as well as how social relations are negotiated, modified, challenged and reproduced."
> COMPAS 2011

In this chapter we refer to our assumption that working migrants play a crucial role in construction processes in China in general and in Shanghai in particular. We want to broaden the range of the participants by also seeing them as important actors in the construction process. As the subjects of investigation are part of worldwide migration movements, this chapter gives insight into the issues of migration with a special focus on our research field.

In this book we are focusing on two social groups: rural working migrants and international business migrants. Within the vast field of migration, we are particularly interested in working migration within the construction industry – people who are involved in shaping the urban space in China. Explicitly, we are focusing on peasant migrants who come to the city to work on construction sites as construction workers on the one hand, and on the other hand we are observing Western business migrants who come to Shanghai to work in the construction business mainly as planners, designers, managers, and builders. Both groups are involved in the construction process, but at quite different stages of the process. Whereas the construction workers are executers, responsible for manually erecting the buildings, the global migrants are in most cases active in a management and supervising postion. Therefore, rural migrant workers usually contribute hard skills and global migrant workers provide specialized knowledge during the building process.

This juxtaposition is of course a simplification of the much more complex realm of urban production. In the context of this work, when dealing with working migration within the construction process, we can only reveal certain aspects, but we will not be able to adequately explain the complete phenomenon. We are thus just opening a small window on a large issue, as this is an examination of a very specific topic within the broad field of current urban transformations in China and the therefore interrelated phenomena of working migration. Box 3 provides an overview of the definitions relevant for this book.

Box 3: People in Motion

- Tourism
  people travelling, indulging consciously in not working
- Travellers
  tourists travelling open ended, longer, appreciating the "real culture" of a place, often travelling unplanned
- Volunteer Tourists
  with the goal to "interact with the culture" working for pleasure, combining tourism and work
  similar: exchange students or students travelling to do field work abroad
- Other Tourists
  technical consultants, missionaries and social-sector personnel, trips taken to attend conferences, do field work or provide consultations by academics
- Business Travellers
  sent by their company or on their own not for leisure, trips may be long or short, involve familiarity with the culture visited and the local language or not, and require sociability or not
  sometimes have homes or "home bases" in more than one place
- Professional "Travellers"
  sports professionals, singers, musicians, actors, salespeople, sailors, soldiers, airline and train personnel, commercial fishermen, farm workers, long-distance truck drivers
- Itinerant
  individuals travelling from place to place with no fixed home
  e.g. Pilgrims, Sadhus (Jain monks from India)
- Refugees
  forced to mobility, a person in fear of being persecuted for reasons of race, religion, nationality, membership of a particular social group or political opinion

- Nomads
  traditional way of gaining livelihood includes mobility, communities of people moving from place to place
  hunter-gatherer (following seasons like the Hadza in Tanzania)
  pastoral nomads (raising herds like Bedouins of the Arabic desert, Indigenous peoples of the Americas)
  peripatetic nomads (offering a craft or trade when moving among settled populations)
  recently also used describing a broad range of individuals with an ongoing movement in their lives (see chapter Urban Nomads)

Source. Agustìn 2003; Stiglechner 2009; COMPAS 2011; IOM 2010

2.1 Labour Migration

The unequal distribution of opportunities in the world is one of the main driving forces for people on the move, and movement is the very essence of migration. According to the UN DESA (2013) there are 232 million international migrants equal to 3.2 per cent of the world's population, and internal migrants worldwide – migrants inside of their country of origin – account for 763 million migrants. This brings the total number of migrants to just under 1 billion worldwide today.

As there are so many different kinds of people on the move – tourists, business travellers, refugees, and migrants – what especially defines a migrant? While all the groups outlined in Box 3 have very different reasons for their beeing on the move, the UNDP generally defines a migrant as an individual who has changed their usual place of residence, either by crossing an international border or moving within their country of origin to another region, district, or municipality. According to UN statistics a migrant is an individual who has resided in a foreign country for more than one year. Those travelling for shorter periods, such as tourists and businesspeople, are not considered migrants. However, common usage includes certain types of shorter-term migrants, such as seasonal farm-workers and other temporary workers. Migration in many cases is related to work, but when we use the terms labour migration, job migration, or working migration we are stressing the fact that work is the key driver for migration. A migrant worker is defined as "person who is to be engaged, is engaged, or has been engaged in a remunerated activity in a State of which he or she is not a national" by the UN Convention on the Rights of Migrants, but the term is also used for individuals migrating within their country (UN General Assembly 1990:

A/RES/45/158). Migration includes a major, permanent, and completed move from one location to another.

Box 4: Migration

> - Internal Migration / Temporary Working Migration
>   greater economic security through seasonal or temporary mobility
>   migrants are often exposed to hazardous circumstances (such as abusive employers, illegality, exploitation by middle men) and to danger, risk of injury and illness
> - Global Labour Mobility / International Business Migration
>   global demand for labour as an effect of globalization – a well known phenomenon with a new impact
>   the renewed interest in temporary, rather than permanent mobility has been caused by fears about the practical and political consequences of permanent settlement of migrants and the rapid urbanization
> - Skilled Migration – International and Internal
>   a synonym for legal, permanent migration
>   the richest countries and regions compete with each other to fill structural labour shortages in an increasingly knowledge-based economy, also called "brain gain" as opposed to "brain drain"[1]
> - Forced Migration
>   forced displacement is often accompanied by a processes of impoverishment
>   usually viewed as problem, rather than to make the best of their adverse conditions and mobilize around their rights like refugees or oustees[2]
>   civil war-induced migration (see Refugees in Box 3)
> - Return Migration
>   return of refugees after the end of conflict, skilled professionals who contribute to a country's development, or rejected asylum-seekers and irregular migrants

---

1 Brain Gain: Immigration of trained and talented individuals into the destination country, brain drain: emigration of individuals with special skills or knowledge
2 Oustee - a person who is ousted, especially one who is removed from his place of residence or land to make room for infrastructure improvement or a public works project. Many forced displacements entail loss of working environment and social community.

> return migrants from overseas to Mainland China are called *haigui* – literally meaning "return from overseas". Interestingly, the returnees are also called "Sea Turtles", a term that has the same pronunciation as *haigui* in Chinese pinyin. Sea turtles depart from their place of birth, travel for a certain period of time and will eventually return to their place of origin[3]

Source. Categories based on The Development Research Centre on Migration, Globalisation and Poverty (DRC) 2011; Huang Yedan 2008; IOM 2010; UNDP 2009

As shown in Box 4 the reasons for movement and migration are manifold. In the context of this book, when we speak of international migrants, we are referring exclusively to the incoming foreign migration flow. Chinese living abroad or Chinese returning from overseas (see Box 4 Return Migrants, the *haigui*) are not included. When we speak of internal migration we refer to the particular Chinese phenomenon of rural working migration.

2.2 LABOUR MIGRATION IN CHINA

> "The journey from farm to city is the story of China's transformation from a poor and backward country to a global economic superpower."
> MILLER 2012:1

The focus of the debate on labour migration flows is shifting to China. Clearly the country with the highest population in the world has an impact on global human movements. Today masses of rural migrant workers are flocking into Chinese cities even though the government of China maintains restrictions on internal movement. Migration in China, with all its possibilities and obstacles, is inevitably connected to the national household registration system – the hukou (户口) system. Nevertheless, migrant flows have a major impact on China's development and rural to urban migration in particular is "rapidly reshaping economic, demographic and social landscapes of the Chinese city and countryside"

---

[3] *Haigui* play an important role in China's urban transformation and are another phenomenon – in addition to global and rural urban nomads – that is worthy of further consideration. For further information see Return migration: a case study of "sea turtles" in Shanghai by Huang Yedan, 2008.

(Fan 2008: 1). The exact total number of "migrants in their own country" is uncertain (ibid.). In 2006 the number of people not living and working in places where they were registered was estimated to be about 150 million, accounting for about 12% of China's population (NBS 2007). In 2014 the China Statistical Yearbook puts the quantity of internal migrants as high as 253 million. This means that they are living in the city without an urban *hukou*, and are thus part of the floating population.

The national household registration system – the *hukou* system "[...]has not only fortified institutional and social barriers between rural and urban China but also influenced all aspects of Chinese society and economy" (Fan 2008: 40). "This system determines the movement of individuals by dividing China's population into rural and urban citizens. The separation between hukou registration place and the actual living place, is a unique phenomenon in Chinese cities." (cf. Shi Li 2010; Fan 2008; HDR China 2008; Friedmann 2005)

Figure 8: Internal Migration in China

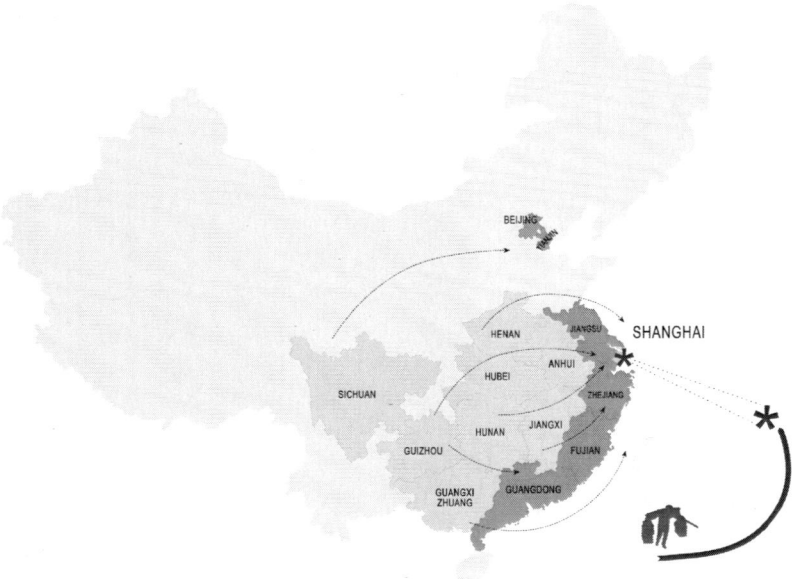

Source. Illustration Bronner | Reikersdorfer, based on Chinese National Bureau of Statistics 2014

"By maintaining an institutional and social order in which peasants are inferior to urbanites, and by permitting peasants to work in urban areas as 'temporary' migrants – migrants that are denied urban hukou and entitlements – the state has created a migrant labor regime that enables labor-intensive industrialization and urban development. In this way, the state makes available a large supply of rural labor to advance its developmentalist strategy at low cost and at the same time ensures that most peasant migrants will eventually return to the countryside without burdening the state. These peasant migrants are attractive to global investors." (Fan 2008: 4)

To understand contemporary China, in which the dynamics between the East and the West and between capitalism and socialism are not easily categorized, it is useful to situate the development of China within a broader historical context. The pre-conditions for the mechanism of the contemporary production of space are strongly connected to the past.

A Historical Overview

"The modern in China is consequently contradictory and complex in nature, not simply a linear move from one historical moment to the next and certainly not a Wiggish progress from communism to capitalism." (Keith 2011: 402)

Mao's China

After the revolution in 1949 the policy of the Chinese Communist Party (CCP) under the leadership of Mao Zedong was "industrialization without much urbanization" (Naughton 1995 in Chen/Clark 2006). The development of infrastructure, public transport, electricity and social services for cities was considered by the CCP to be time-consuming and expensive. Therefore, the focus was on creating smaller, less costly urban centres in inland regions closer to the supply of resources (Chen/Clark 2006). To promote the "collective life" they established people's communes as large collective farms and by 1965, 97 percent of the national labour force consisted of rural workers (Friedmann in Brigde/Watson 2011).

During the Maoist period state agencies allocated jobs and transferred workers from one job to another through "unified state assignment" to control labor migration (Fan 2008: 45). A similar logic was present when the CCP went even further and implemented the household registration system to control individual movement into the cities in the late 1950s. Since then China's household registration system has identified each person as a resident of a particular area.

The hukou system divided Chinese society into urban citizens and rural citizens. It effectively put a stop to rural to urban migration as it subjects all Chinese residents to strict control through registration at their place of residence. As a consequence, only state-mandated mass movements were possible. Urbanites were entitled to work and had access to housing, education, and other social services. Food was subsidized with *liangpiao* (粮票, food coupons) which, along with hospital treatments, were bound to their designated *hukou*. Open markets were virtually non-existent, as almost all necessities in urban areas were controlled by the state. Without an urban *hukou* and the accompanying benefits it was nearly impossible to survive in the city.

During the Great Leap Forward (1958-60) mass rural movement into the cities was prescribed to rapidly increase the size of the economy, and during the Cultural Revolution (1966-76) urban youth were forced to move to the countryside. The impact on society was immense and directly or indirectly touched essentially all of China's population. While the original village was a rural society integrated by strict family ties, the arrival of migrant populations dismantled the traditional village structure and was resulted in the fragmentation of village social space (Wu Fulong in Brigde/Watson 2011). Until 1980 the *hukou* system was inviolate, making it impossible for people to seek employment elsewhere or to move in order to pursue educational opportunities or better public services.

When dealing with the history of Chinese urbanization it is useful to take a look at a second powerful tool that controlled individual movement, particularly in urban areas: the state-owned work units known as *danwei*. During the Great Leap Forward (1958-60), millions left agricultural work and crowded into the cities to work in industrial occupations, which caused the collapse of the food production chain and led to mass starvation and hunger. "Out of this immense catastrophe emerged a new set of economic conditions, which created the foundations for the Chinese danwei system" (Naughton 1995: 172). The *danwei* provided employment, housing, health care, and social services for its members but in return required compliance with the political and economic opinion of the enterprises and the state. Residents lived, worked, and socialized within the work unit space. Through the urban *danwei*, the state controlled urban society and also encouraged residents to be active participants in the party (Bray 2009). Parallels can be drawn to socialist cities in the former Soviet Union, where the state-run workplace had a central position in everyday life (Bradshaw/Stenning 2004). During the 1960s when the *danwei* system was most highly developed, the absence of labor mobility was the most important characteristic of the Chinese economy (Naughton 1995). Both the *hukou* and the *danwei* systems can be seen as socialist instruments that controlled and minimized the movement of Chinese citizens (cf. Chen/Clark 2006).

Due to the aforementioned restrictions large cities showed almost no growth from the mid-1960s until the late 1970s. Bray speaks of Chinese cities as a collection of self-contained and spatially defined communities rather than as an integrated urban network. This is clearly evident on the basis of closed neighbourhoods and gated communities that are surrounded by walls, gates, and fences (Hassenpflug 2010). "Consequently, from 1960 onwards, city planning was suspended. Though sporadically resumed in the early 1970s, it did not regain its full influences and power until the following decade when China, in another historical turn, was in a rush to 'marketize' its economy" (Bray 2009: 124).

Prior to China's opening in the 1980s, housing was mainly provided by the state in the planned economy through the welfare-oriented public housing distribution system. The living area of a family was assigned by the number of family members, rents were paid in a symbolic way, and as a consequence homes were equipped according to the minimum living standard (Zhang Xiaochung in Brigde/Watson 2011). Chinese urbanism during the socialist period can be described as uniform and collective (Wu Fulong in Brigde/Watson 2011).

Post-Mao China

After the death of Mao Zedong in 1978 a comprehensive transformation of mainland China began. The Chinese term *xia hai* (下海) – entering the sea – represents this period. China started to participate in global economic markets, shifted from a planned to a market economy, and became defined by "market socialism" (cf. McMillan/Naughton 1996). "Disempowerment of the nation-state in the fact of increasingly flexible and mobile capital, in China we see a process of negotiation between the state and new kinds of economic actors" (Anagost 1997 in Chen/Clark 2006: 10). Nevertheless political power remained with the CCP, while a system of bureaucratic power (the state) executed laws and regulations based on the five-year plan. This is still the case today. In practice it means that an ambivalent relationship exists between the capitalist practices of the production of space and strong state interference (Friedmann 2005; Pun Ngai/ Xu Yi 2011).

In the early 1980s the reformer and leader of the CCP Deng Xiaoping moved to reduce the distinction between rural and urban through a liberalization of the *hukou* system and allowed migrants to move to the cities with temporary residence permits tied to their work contracts. This had a major impact on China's rapid urbanization as migration was now allowed to take place and led to mass movements of millions of peasants throughout China. The large-scale mobility has dramatically transformed rural and urban social space (Chen/Clark 2006). By loosening the key controls of socialist economies like bureaucratic planning and distribution, and centralized control over the production process, the new reforms not only brought along progress but also uncertainty, insecurity, and instability. After the removal of communal protection, state support, and shared facilities, peasant families in particular were responsible for themselves. This led to a new situation that brought along with it much dissatisfaction regarding how to support one's family. The enormous scope of the rural-urban migration from the 1980s into the 1990s and beyond has been characterized as "a period of great migration" and as "one of the most prominent demographic events in twentieth-century China" (Zai Liang 2006: 499).

However, parallel to this internal migration, China opened up and began to participate in global markets. In order to attract foreign direct investment (FDI) China introduced Special Economic Zones (SEZs) in five harbour cities along the coast in the early 1980s (Xiamen, Fujian province; Shantou, Guangdong province; Shenzhen, Guangdong province; Zhuhai, Guangdong province; and Hainan province). Compared to the rest of China, the SEZs are characterized by more free-market-oriented laws including tax allowances. In 1984 China further opened 14 coastal cities to overseas investment in including Shanghai. At this point foreigners entered the market, including the housing market. Nowadays one can find a high density of foreign settlements in and around these SEZs (Li Xiangning/Zhang Xiachun 2008).

2.3 THE INTERNATIONAL BUSINESS MIGRANT

As shown previously, the discourse on labour migration in China in particular deals with internal migrants moving from rural to urban areas. The word migrant is nearly always used in reference to the working class. But there is another flow of migrants who are typically not labelled as migrants: International business migrants, better known as expats, who move around the world from one working place to another. Expat is short for expatriate, and the word expatriate comes from Latin and means being outside the native country. So their key driver for migration is also work, but the circumstances are completely different. Brought about by rapid globalization, the increasing demand for a mobile work force is leading to a new phenomenon within our society. A new population group linked to this new mobility has emerged: people who are moving to cities to live and work from all over the world. Highly skilled professionals can work anywhere in the world due to the advent of mobile computing, even in cafés, airports, and trains. Combining business and leisure is a well-practiced concept. In Shanghai alone there were 176,000 resident foreigners registered in 2013 according to the Shanghai Statistical Yearbook 2014.

The ways in which business and rural migrants are perceived and represented by local urbanites and by the mainstream published media are quite unequal. International migrants are usually perceived as individuals realizing their identities (Beynon 2008). Internal migrants on the other hand have the image of being rootless instead of flexible. In this context of obvious differences Saskia Sassen speaks of knowledge workers as opposed to hard skill workers. The differences between the two groups are especially visible in the extreme inequalities seen in cities. To her, it is this distinction of knowledge based and manual work that really distinguishes rural migrant workers and international business workers, rather than how they are perceived (Sassen in Burdett/Sudjic 2011: 59).

Figure 9: International Migration to China

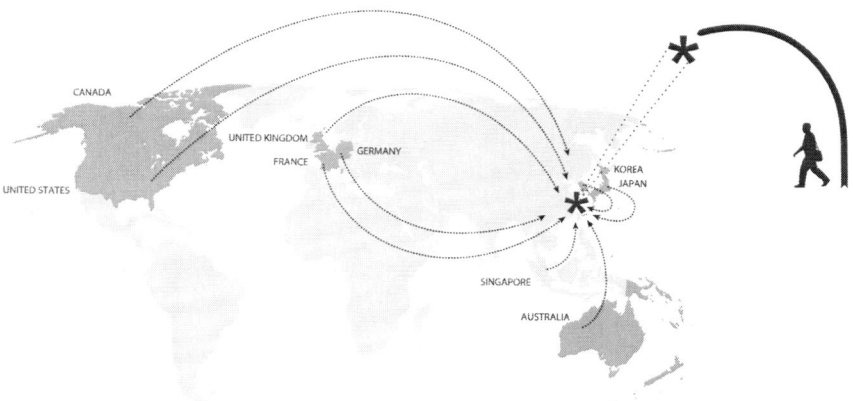

Source. Illustration Bronner | Reikersdorfer, based on Shanghai Statistical Yearbook 2014.

2.4 A Peculiarity: the Similarities

Despite the many obvious differences between rural and global migrants, upon closer examination there are a surprising number of similarities that characterize these two social groups. At first glance they do not seem to be comparable, but a closer look reveals that they have an astonishing number of parallels. Below the surface of these seemingly unrelated groups, there exists a driving mechanism which makes them closely resemble one another.

Although they seem very different, both international and internal migrants can be referred to as labour migrants, as they move to a new place in order to work. Both extremely well-paid and extremely low-wage workers are characterized by this highly mobile lifestyle (Ladewig/Mellinger 2003; Sassen in Burdett/Sudjic 2011). They are both highly mobile and flexible, and often never really settle down. They are constantly searching for new opportunities, particularly in relation to work. Internal and international migrants reflect the fact that mobility is not only a natural part of human history but a continuing dimension of development and of modern societies. In Western literature people on the move are portrayed as individuals, constantly seeking to connect to emerging opportunities and changing their circumstances accordingly (Beynon 2008). They are detached from their society of origin, and they influence the host society. A large number of people in both destination and source places are affected by the movement of migrants through flows of money, knowledge, and ideas (HDR 2008).

What effect do migrants bring to the local people and how do they influence society in the long term? Sociologists speak of specific effects that migrants have on their place of origin caused by their departure and on their destination caused by their arrival. Migrants are disadvantaged and at the same time also benefit from their situation, but they usually have a stronger perception of the disadvantages (Luft/Schimany 2010). They are part of the so-called immigration society at the same time as being part of the emigration society. Migrating individuals have effects on the society of origin and simultaneously on the receiving society. One of these measurable effects is the transfer of money by foreign workers to the home country – the remittances. Remittances from migrants significantly exceeded international aid in 2010 (DESA 2011). These funds also have an effect internally in that they help to reduce poverty in rural China.

Figure 10: Societies Influenced by Migration

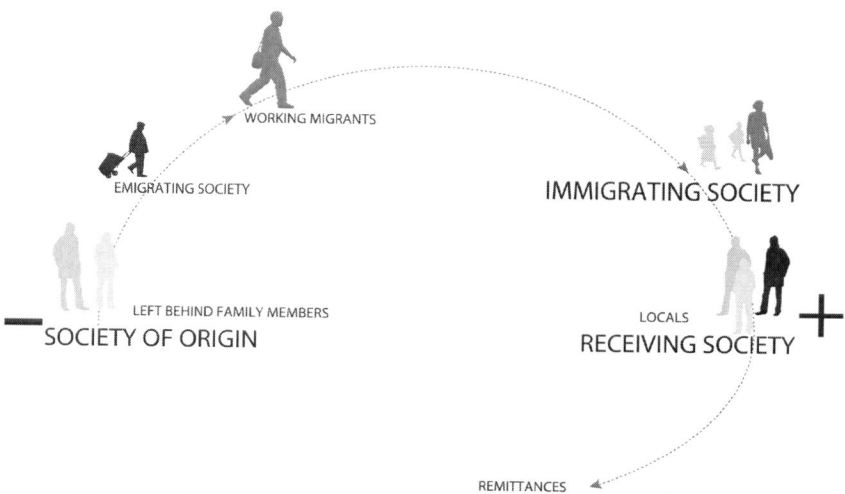

Source. Illustration Bronner | Reikersdorfer 2011

To us these boundaries between the many elements of society who mingle in the city due to their work demonstrate the immediacy of the problem and negatively affect the quality of life in the city. Through their movement they are actively causing social change and have a significant impact on the receiving society, but at the same time they are affected by the reaction of the receiving society.

3. Urban Nomads

Permanently Temporary

> "We are as it were like large knitting (or perhaps sewing machine) needles, stitching ourselves into the local fabric of the environs, grounding and rooting ourselves, even if only momentarily."
> MACAULEY 2002: 196

In this chapter we will introduce an alternative concept of human mobility. It is our objective to create a shift in the perception of the observed groups from passive, victimized migrants to active participants in urban life. Within the ongoing sociospatial transformations in China we investigate two completely different groups, which at the same time have many similarities. We observe them in parallel rather than comparatively. Rural and global migration exists simultaneously, the affected groups are temporary urban citizens, and both face their threats and challenges. But above all – and this is what makes this observation so relevant in the discourse on migration – they are permanently temporary urban citizens with unique explicit and implicit spatial needs. They repeatedly change their habitat according to their work as they move from place to place. And in this continuous life phase of moving, rural and global migrants constantly seek to connect to emerging opportunities and change their circumstances accordingly. While most migration studies focus on social circumstances, our observations emphasize the social and spatial nature of migration.

Migrants are a social group seemingly excluded from concepts celebrating repeated movement, such as cosmopolitanism and transnationalism. By trying to maintain something of the past while remaining open to the future, migrants often show great strength and demonstrate the ability to creatively adapt to new situations (Agustín 2003). To highlight these capabilities, to underline the uniqueness of these permanent temporary livelihoods, and to avoid victimization we suggest a new name for the two social groups observed in this book. This term should empower them to recognize their potential.

Rural working migrants and international business migrants who are temporarily involved in construction processes are at the same time participants in the city. While they are active in shaping the city through the projects they are working on, they are also individuals living in the city. This leads to a double role of the observed. By trying to achieve a transformation of just being involved to being participants in urban society, even if only temporarily, we will call them Urban Nomads. Urban, because the phenomenon is particular to the urban environment and nomads, to make a clear distinction between people who have made one or many major moves which are complete and those who are in recurrent temporary living situations caused by their work, for example by the unsteady nature of construction projects. Deleuze and Guattari argue that the nomad is "deterritorialized par excellence" (2004 [1987]: 380) while the migrant entails reterritorialization after moving. Explicitly, we aim to highlight and observe how urban nomads interact with space, as well as how social issues are implicated in this interaction.

It is with these characteristics of urban nomads in mind, we will take a closer look at the existing debate on contemporary nomads. In the 17th century the word nomad described people living outside the city who moved from place to place and were not tied to royal or state violence. Traditional nomads "engage in periodic and cyclical movement for specific purposes, at defined times and across particular territories, dictated by climate, vegetation, and the habits of animals that they rear or hunt" (Beynon 2008: 13). They usually move as a community, which leads to strong ties within their group. Traditional nomadism is thus a way of life in which a community has an organized rotation of settlements that correspond to the usage of natural resources.

In contrast peripatetic nomads, who are more common in industrialized nations, usually travel unaccompanied from place to place offering their trade wherever they go. Their characteristics of travelling as individuals and for work correlate with the urban nomads observed in this book. Although the key feature of the notion of cities is permanent settlement, most urban citizens are, to some extent, nomadic (Burdett/Sudjic 2011). Our lives have become punctuated by mobility whether it is in a geographical or an intellectual way. Travel has become such an important part of everyday life that we are permanently moving – for business or pleasure, whether it be short or long distances or relocation. As definitions of nomads are varied, we recognize that there are a number of different types of nomadic groups within our society. Even though these concepts follow quite different paths, the examples of urban nomads all have in common that temporary phases of life are performed repeatedly. Urban nomads are therefore individuals without a perceived permanent domicile, living in "pockets of residual space" that change and transform through time (Wrightsman 2007). They are strongly differentiated by socio-economic circumstances (Craven/Morelli 2004). Hence we identify with the spatial qualities of nomadism – together with migration, which is usually discussed in connection with social issues – rather than the "self-celebration of postmodern intellectuals as nomadic 'wandering stars' as is emphasized in certain nomadic discourses" (Pels 1999: 76).

These conceptualizations of urban nomads have the two key implications for us – global and rural urban nomads as subject of the present investigation. Due to the difficulty of capturing nomads with census surveys and similar recording methods, we will focus more on their qualitative circumstances. By choosing a qualitative approach to gain insights we seek to have the chance to explore an in-depth understanding of the implicit and explicit needs of the observed groups. And while nomadism as discussed is a global phenomenon, most of the scholarly literature thus far is rooted in Western perspectives. Thus we have to correlate this understanding of urban nomads with perspectives from China and Shanghai in particular. It is important to point out that nomadism formerly arose out of necessity, and only later occurred for purposes of entertainment and lifestyle.

"While many of us lead lives that are, in part, nomadic, the circumstances influencing such an existence are often varied. For some it may be a conscious decision, while for others there is simply no choice. A person may work in a nomadic fashion but return to their home periodically. Others, such as the homeless, may live completely outside the equation of house=home." (Craven/Morelli 2004: 1)

The much larger change is that in the past – and in some situations still today – no one really needed to take nomads into account as they lived outside of cities and took their traditions with them from place to place. But today's nomads have a much greater impact on society; urban nomads live scattered throughout the city amidst settled people. The proximity to one another of these different lifestyles represents a whole different challenge for the creation of an equitable urban environment.

3.1 Emerging Challenges in Migration Studies

According to census figures by the Chinese National Bureau of Statistics (NBS 2010), China had 1.34 billion inhabitants by 2010, accounting for almost 20% of the world's population. When speaking about China the focus is often on numbers and statistics as the country is "the land of superlatives". Although this enormous size suggests great potential in many areas, in the case of migration "there are several reasons why all estimates of the numbers of migrants are suspect" (Friedmann 2005: 64). He argues that there is no clear definition, a repeated counting of the same migrant at different points, a failure to distinguish between different lengths of stay of migrants, and an impossibility of estimating the number of unregistered migrants.

Due to this circumstances, an interdisciplinary approach is essential to observing urban change qualitatively rather than quantitatively. As much as we are impressed by the scale of the urban phenomena in China, it becomes clear that the increasing complexity of social relations cannot be explained only by numbers and statistics. Based on Lefebvre's (2003 [1970]: 46) descriptive methods we can only "reveal certain aspects" but won't be able to adequately explain social relations. When the urban phenomenon is broken down into several categories – such as the number of urban dwellers – in order to be analyzed separately, a particular situation rather than the phenomenon as a whole will be captured. "Every specialized science cuts from the global phenomenon a 'field' or 'domain', which it illuminates in its own way" (ibid.: 48). And further, each science is divided in several sub-disciplines.

According to this principle numbers and statistics are an important part of understanding the urban phenomena highlighted in this work, and will support observations by emphasizing their size. But they are unable to capture the entire urban migration process as it relates to the complexity of construction processes in China. "It is far more convenient to approach the global [reality] through a series of levels and stages – a difficult procedure, for with each step we risk running into various obstacles and mazes" (ibid.: 48). Therefore the many snapshots from different perspectives are an attempt to offer a comprehensive picture, and our interdisciplinary approach is essential in our attempts to grasp the complexity of the urban phenomenon.

3.2 TAILOR-MADE CITY PLANNING AND COCOONED LIVING

Referencing critical urban studies, we have discussed in detail how space is not just an object, but rather is a societal process of production. Further, we have illustrated how relationships and dependencies during construction processes are detailed in project management, and we have highlighted that beyond the traditional participants in the case of China we are confronted with another social group within the construction process: Internal and international working migrants. As rural and global working migrants are play a special role in the building industry in Shanghai we have called for a shift in perception to acknowledge the perpetual temporariness and other related spatial needs. The title "urban nomads" thus clarifies the human-oriented approach of our investigation. It is with the intention of providing a critical perspective on this subject that this chapter focuses on our core questions for the two case studies and subsequent observations. In doing so we remain mindful of the theoretical framework we introduced in the previous four chapters as we build on the concepts that have been introduced.

Therefore, if the city is a societal process, if construction is more than the built final result, if migration plays an important role within construction processes in Shanghai, and if temporary migrants should be treated as full urban citizens, what then are the specific challenges, needs and experiences for urban nomads in the city? What are the particularities of their role within the urban realm? What are the specific, actual needs of urban nomads during the construction process – spatially and thus also socially? How should a person who is permanently moving claim his or her rights in the city? Is he or she doomed to be deprived and to remain discontent? What does it mean for the city spatially that an enormous number of people are only temporary residents? What are the effects of urban nomads participating in the construction process? And what are the responsibilities of future city planners in this context?

Following on the underlying conceptions and questions discussed here, we will conduct the two case studies on global and rural urban nomads by putting forward some core arguments. This study is written from a perspective of critical urban studies and, more precisely, from the standpoint of architectural investigation embedded in a social discourse on the on-going practice of construction in China. These arguments are geared primarily toward architects, urban planners, and designers who work with the Chinese construction industry or intend to work with it in the future. It is our objective to raise awareness of the two target groups by portraying them in various snapshots taken during multiple stays in

China and especially during the period of research for this book in fall, 2010 and professional working experience from 2013-2015. By keeping in mind the dynamics of social change in contemporary urban China when analyzing construction sites and planning practices in Shanghai, we are able to maintain an awareness of the big picture while also focusing on details.

The desire for a socially just and sustainable form of urbanization will be the approach that frames our further analyse. Here, we reference three different spatial layers: the urban scale, the living environment, and building projects.

Figure 11: Large Scale – Urban Scale – The Excluded User

Source. Bronner | Reikersdorfer 2011

Hypothesis 1: Tailor-Made City Planning

Urban space in Shanghai is transforming rapidly but urban planners don't consider temporary residents in their city planning concepts. Thus, rural and global nomads do not feel that they are an inherent part of the city. Moreover, they become permanent outsiders instead of urban participants.

Figure 12: Medium Scale – Living Environment – The Excluded Consumer

Source. Bronner | Reikersdorfer 2011

Hypothesis 2: Cocooned Living

Foreigners from around the world and people from other regions tend to cluster when moving to a city. In Shanghai this habit of residential concentration of particular groups is even more pronounced, as can be seen in residential dwellings.

Figure 13: Small Scale – Bulding Projects – Intersections Between the Involved

Source. Bronner | Reikersdorfer 2011

Hypothesis 3: Working Challenges

The completely different educational backgrounds of the rural and global working migrants participating in the construction process result in a challenging situation that neither group is adequately prepared for. This is reflected not only in the quality of construction but also in communication difficulties during the construction process.

Figure 14: Analytical Frame – Production of Space

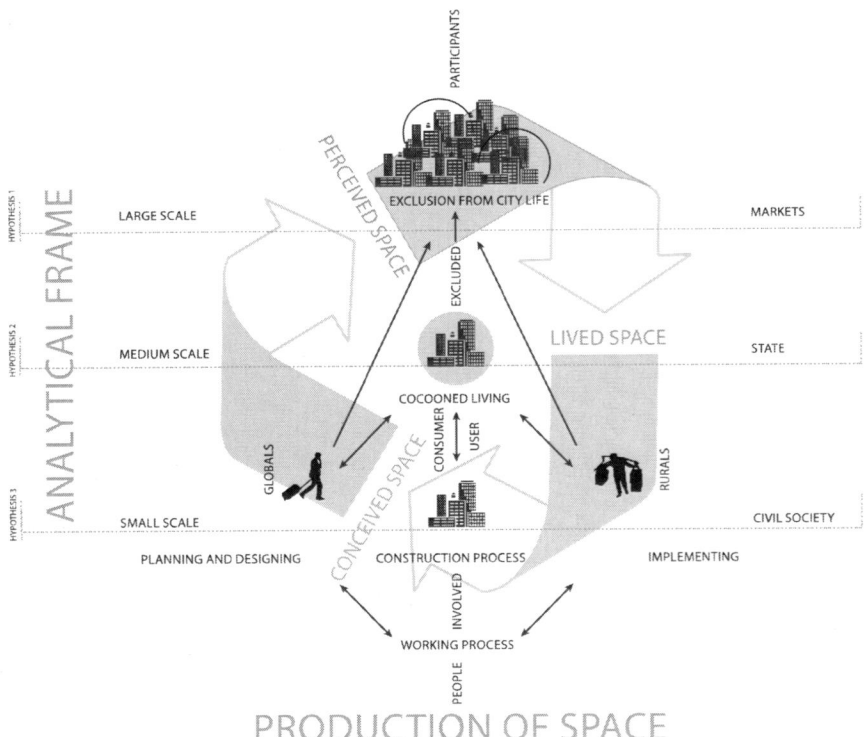

Source. Illustration Bronner | Reikersdorfer 2011

Research Approach and Objectives

To elaborate and test our hypotheses these three spatial levels represent the research framework for our analysis within dynamic urban space in Shanghai. We have taken a dialectic-discursive approach: on the one hand we examine local internal working migration, and on the other hand we look at the phenomenon of global migration within the Chinese construction industry. The results are not directly compared, but rather give an understanding of their circumstances. A draw on a qualitative approach to portray a socio-spatial reality in order to identify the transformation process, and to further understand the different perspectives of those involved. Therefore, we have collected the stories of individuals and viewed them in context in order to comprehend the big picture of urban transformation in Shanghai.

Further, we are drawing on three theoretical strands from the disciplines of urban studies, project management and migration studies. We intend to include the emergence of spaces through social action in our observations of construction processes. According to Knierbein "dimensions left out in empirical studies should be then afterwards contextualized again and further blind spots and newly emerging questions for further research should offer spaces in transition during urbanization processes" (Knierbein 2010: 401). But as the studied phenomenon has repeated itself time after time, these sequences become relevant objects of observation. After gaining scientific insight on particular mechanisms and phenomena of the production of space, these descriptions can be confronted with normative positions to increase awareness and sensitize ongoing debates (ibid.).

Hence, our interest lies in social action and the personal circumstances of the people involved in construction. Here, a shift from being involved to being a participant on the construction site and from being excluded to being included in city life – in essence, being a person who shapes the city and takes an active part in it – is desirable, but perhaps still an utopian vision. According to Lefebvre utopias are sometimes necessary to induce social change.

"By seeking to point the way towards a different space, towards the space of a different (social) life and of a different mode of production, this project [a strategic hypothesis] straddles the breach between science and utopia, reality and ideality, conceived and lived. It aspires to surmount these oppositions by exploring the dialectical relationship between 'possible' and 'impossible', and this both objectively and subjectively." (Lefebvre 2009 [1974]: 60)

On the other hand, project management studies have analyzed in detail the organization of construction processes, but have not yet considered sufficiently the social processes imbedded therein. The discipline of project management describes the production of material space as a process driven by the three key variables of time, cost, and quality, and has defined the positions of participants involved in the process. The focus is usually on a smooth progression of work on the site and on important interfaces between different disciplines. However, on the construction site more than just material space is produced. The process of construction needs to be linked to the much larger process of the production of social space, including perceived, conceived, and lived space as defined by Lefebvre. In China, construction workers actually live on site, which makes the building site a lived space, adding a whole new layer to the traditional operations at a site.

Our objective is to challenge the status quo of the production of space relevant to both theory and practice. Clearly, our focus here is limited to the interests of the observed groups, but we are confident that we can demonstrate the potential for improvement in certain respects. Increasingly, the built environment will be premised upon being dynamic, temporary, and portable. As the arguments in this book are situated in three different levels of space, we will consider these different scales when observing rural and global urban nomads in the two case studies. Our investigation is conducted in two parallel parts: the first observes international working migrants and the second looks at internal migrant construction workers. Both are temporarily involved in construction processes in Shanghai and are at the same time participants in the city. While they are active in shaping the city through the projects they are working on, they are also individuals living in the city.

4. Shanghai – Head of the Concrete Dragon

Figure 15: Shanghai, View on Pudong.

Source. Bronner | Reikersdorfer 2008

Chinese urbanism in general and in Shanghai in particular is happing at a tremendous pace. Today the transformation of urban space in Shanghai is manifested not only in a flood of new construction, but also in the change of urban culture and the lifestyle of residents, including their attitude towards life, consumption behavior, and political outlook (Schein 2006). The research field Shanghai as the head of the "concrete dragon" (Campanella 2008), is a global city with over 23 million inhabitants (NBS 2011) with 14 million registered and nine million floating inhabitants without a proper *hukou* registration. A city that is constantly negotiating what it means to be modern and what it means to be Chinese (Keith 2011). References to historical development and the interweaving of Chinese and foreigners in Shanghai reveal a complex urban conglomerate that reflects sharp contrasts in the build environment and within its social patterns (Logan 2002). This creates the very particular framework for our case study. Regarding the three layers of space – the urban scale, the living environment, and building projects – observations in Shanghai are presented in the following chapters.

4.1 Urban Transformation in Shanghai

As the economic powerhouse of China, Shanghai is and always has been a point of intersection between East and the West. The power of global interconnectedness through trade and investment flows has shaped the city since the opening of the treaty port in 1843. Ever since that time Shanghai has had an intimate relationship with foreign communities and has enjoyed locational advantages that derive from its status as a "gateway" (Bergère 2010). Shanghai's first International Settlements were British, resulting from the terms of the Treaty of Nanking at the end of the First Opium War in 1842, followed by an American and French presence. At that time it had already become obvious that the majority of foreigners tended to settle in certain areas in Shanghai, which remains the case today. The international influence of the settlements can still be seen in the contemporary cityscape. Modern commercial and industrial development led to rapid growth of the population in the second half of the 19th century. The compressed *lilong* house, which is representative of this period of urbanization and commercialization, was a reaction to the increasing density of Shanghai and the resulting new living requirements. It represents a mixture of European terraced housing design and concrete, brick, and stone and the traditional Chinese courtyard house and can be seen as an example of how the urban fabric has reacted to new demands and needs over time (Balfour/Zheng 2002). During Shanghai's golden age in the 1920s, with a population over two million, "the Paris of the Orient" was "a meeting ground for people from all countries, a great and a unique city, one of the most remarkable in the world" (Pott 1928 in Gugler 2004: 28). Fascinated by the dynamic and international flair of old Shanghai, today primarily foreign historians are coming to terms with the past and probing this time period of foreign influence in terms of its impact on city life and landscape. The relationship between the Chinese and foreigners in Shanghai was significant in the city's development and can be seen as the driving force behind the formation of a unique culture with roots in the West but adapted to the national Chinese culture (Bergère 2010).

After the revolution in 1949 the international atmosphere disappeared immediately and city life changed dramatically. China was transformed into a "closed society", one where central and subnational governments regulated and limited contact with foreigners and had control over global and as well internal movement in and out of the city (Johnston 2010). At the same time the campaign "The Socialist Transformation of Private Housing" was enforced; accordingly, rural farmland was collectivized, businesses were nationalized, and the private market for land and housing was eliminated for the benefit of the national welfare state (Ma/Wu Fulong 2005: 185). This form of social welfare accompanied by employment with guaranteed job security provided by the state was also known as "Iron Rice Bowl" (Naughton 1995). Through restrictions during the course of the collectivization process, the private housing market was eliminated and top-down distribution of housing was implemented (HsingYou-Tian 2010). The resulting changes led to inadequate housing conditions throughout the country (Sommers/Phillips 2010). Large-scale, welfare-oriented public housing settlements were the embodiment of this spatial politics. Following the motto "production first, living conditions later" the state investment in urban housing as a proportion of gross national product (GNP) averaged only 0.78 % from 1949 to 1978 according to urban affairs reviews (Jieming Zhu 2000). After three decades of almost no development in the housing sector, former US diplomatic worker Tess Johnston, a witness to Chinese history, described Shanghai as a "city frozen in time" when she arrived to work at the American Consulate in the early 80s (Johnston 2010).

In 1979, Deng Xiaoping ushered in the modernization of China by implementing economic reforms including the implementation of the housing and land privatization (Wang Xiaoming 2011). On this occasion property and housing reforms were introduced "to minimize the financial burden on the state, to increase economic efficiency of land use and allocation, and to create land as an asset with value" (Sommers/Phillips 2010: 20). Due to the fact that China retained ownership of land but allowed individuals to develop and transfer land, this new building represents "an ingenious measurement of preserving the socialist ideology of ownership while creating a fast growing urban real estate market" (ibid.). Instead of common wealth the modernization of China brought with it new uncertainty for the Chinese population through the evaporation of job security as well as steady income and benefits (Chen/Clark 2006). One strategy that developed from these new circumstances is the stimulation of the construction industry in order to occupy millions of unemployed workers (Wang Xiaoming 2011). "China's economy, with its concentration of steel mills and cement plants, is unusually dependent on its construction sector" (Miller 2012: 123). In less than 20 years the new market has become one of the pillar industries of the local economy and a "skyrocketing" real estate market has emerged in Shanghai (Wang Xiaoming 2011). Chinese urbanism in general and the experience of Shanghai in particular represent the reckless capitalist production of space. However, developments since 2014 have shown that "the sector has softened visibly, reflecting overbuilding across many cities" (IMF 2015: 1).

Shanghai is eager to become a vibrant international metropolis, which has both positive and negative impacts on the city and on city life. With its ongoing rapid urbanization Shanghai faces many challenges, including environmental issues, shortage of energy and raw materials, and infrastructural concerns. Therefore, serious engagement on all different levels and scales will be crucial for planning processes.

4.2 Impacts on the Lived Space

Given the fact that half of the housing area in Shanghai has been built in the past 20 years, Shanghai's constant changing urban pattern is dominated by enormous construction projects and a rapidly increasing population. The scale of China's economic transition and social transformation is evident in its economic growth rates, which average nearly 10 percent per annum over the last 30 years (HDR China 2008). As a result of the continuously growing population new buildings are rising everywhere and are usually in the form of high-rise buildings due to limited land supply in the inner-city.

Figure 16: m² Floor Area in Shanghai by Year

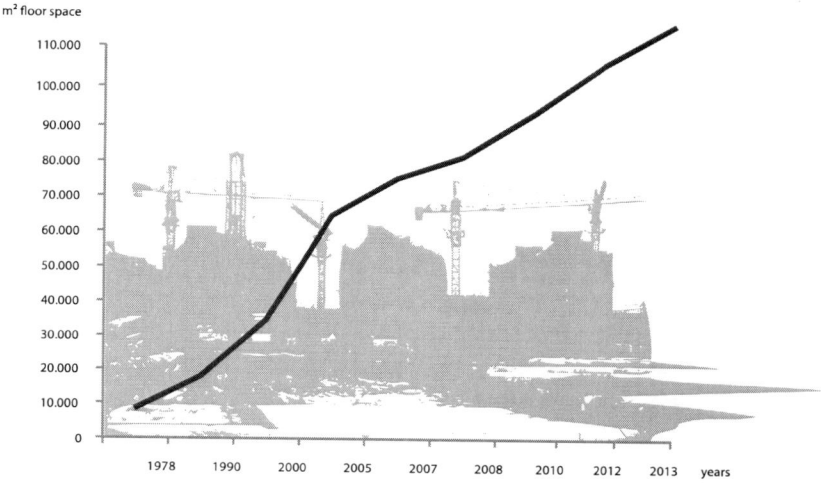

Source. Illustration Bronner | Reikersdorfer, based on Shanghai Statistical Yearbook 2014.

The generic urbanism that we have identified results in a homogenous cityscape (cf. Koolhaas 2004), and it is important not only to consider the spatial consequences of this but also the social effects. As a consequence of the introduction of capitalism, a differentiation between income levels and livelihood has occurred and has led to extreme inequality in living conditions in most Chinese cities. It cannot be ignored that conflicts between the rich and socially vulnerable groups are reinforced by the transformation of old quarters to build high-class neighborhoods for high-income groups. The mass produced high-rise, high-density apartment blocks in Shanghai have succeeded in increasing the amount of personal living space available to citizens. The buildings can be seen as the architectural response to an increasing number of residents; their construction also helps to prevent the formation of accumulation of houses with poor living conditions (Zaera-Polo in Burdett/Sudjic 2011: 336). In "Dreaming of Collective Dwelling in Shanghai" Li Xiangning calls for a new model of social integration along with the city's legendary accumulation of material wealth (Li Xiangning/Zhang Xiaochun 2008: 5). For the metropolitan region of Shanghai, social housing concerns will remain a key issue and the strategy proposed here does not only ensure the continuous use of affordable housing, but also provides the opportunity for buyers to improve their living conditions by purchasing a new house.

Through the high demand for new housing the ongoing urbanization process also profoundly impacts the old city structure. The transformation involves demolition, reshaping, and redevelopment, particularly of old neighborhood quarters. The city government of Shanghai is strongly promoting the transformation of old areas in order to improve the overall quality of housing through the construction of newly built apartments. On the other side there is a growing concern about preserving the character of the old city structure. In particular the foreign community has a nostalgic reference to the former foreign settlements like the French Concession, which maintains a "distinctly cosmopolitan character with a mixture of architecture of past, the present and the future" (Sommers/Philipps 2010: 1). Since 2002 the municipality has paid more attention to historic preservation by passing a law on the protection of cultural relics in order to maintain the city's historic character. Even if much of Shanghai's historic housing stock is in poor condition, and even if it represents an inefficient use of high value space for low-density housing, these old communities are more than just a living space. They contain positive connotations for families and collectives who are helping each other in work and leisure (Hassenpflug 2010). Gentrification and redevelopment of the old neighborhoods further entails marginalization of the displaced residents. Thus relocation often has a huge impact on the everyday life of residents.

4.3 Construction Sites as Research Field

When looking in greater detail at the object of our research – construction sites in and around Shanghai some special features become apparent. Construction sites are situated in the setting of existing urban development; they dominate the changing urban landscape and at the same time are themselves rapidly transforming these spaces. Similar to the observed groups in this study, who are in a permanent state of temporariness, construction sites as a research field are also constantly changing. Thus, like transitory people, the place itself is impermanent. Due to the temporary nature of construction sites, this analysis of building sites and the social organization of the constructions industry may only represent snapshots of a complex process of the production of space. By looking at construction sites as social process we are opening a small window onto a much larger production of urban space.

Therefore, we examine in detail the circumstances of those involved in the following two case studies and link our findings with ideas to action. In both case studies we use terms currently used in the literature to describe the two observed groups in order to position our study within the existing scientific discourse. Thus, in the chapter Global Urban Nomads we use expats and foreigners when writing of international business migrants in Shanghai and migrant workers or the Chinese term *mingong* when describing rural urban nomads from China. The interviews conducted during our research are a snapshot of the construction process at a particular point in time within the process of urban transformation.

5. Global Urban Nomads

> *rù jìng wèn sú* (入境问俗) – when you enter a country enquire about the local customs.
> CHINESE SAYING

The word expatriate implies a person that has the ability to remain mobile, to make the most of their opportunities, and to follow the flows of global commerce. Due to their high level of education and professional skills they have both economic and social capital (Beynon 2008). This chapter includes observations on the phenomenon of clustering of global urban nomads in Shanghai and their impact on the transformation of urban space. Therefore, we illuminate the patterns of organizations of expatriates and describe their lifestyle in their urban surroundings. Further, we compare their different living and working conditions and, beyond this, we illuminate the new challenges and opportunities resulting from cultural differences with which they are confronted in everyday life. We conclude by taking a closer look at the special role of Western architects within the Chinese construction industry, as well as the responsibilities that go along with being an expatriate in general and during the construction process in particular.

5.1 APPROACHING FROM WITHIN

As European researchers we first asked ourselves how we could best approach this topic of working migration within the construction industry in a different cultural setting like China. On the one hand we have the advantage of discovering China and its construction industry through the eyes of outsiders. That gives us the chance to recognize difficulties that those involved do not realize or see anymore because they are surrounded by them every day. On the other hand we were part of the observed group as expatriates. Among other things this allowed us to gain greater insight into the challenging situation of being a global nomad living in a foreign culture. In ethnography these methods can be described as a participatory micro-approach, which is based on the personal experiences of action researchers. "Action researchers, however, are insiders' researchers. They see themselves as part of the situation" (Tornaghi 2009: 35). Part of the research strategy was to be well-connected to the expat's world of Shanghai. We accessed this research field, participated in this world and attended several talks, lectures, and events related to architecture, art, urban planning, and history.

With these issues in mind we approach the subject of global working migration in Shanghai on multiple levels to enable wide-ranging analyses and comparisons. Another research strategy was to conduct several interviews with various experts in the fields of architecture, construction, and design in the professional and academic world. During the interviews we selected questions according to the professional background of our interview partners and adapted the key questions to zoom in on the subject of global working migration. In addition, a descriptive method was used to gather information about the present conditions of global urban nomads. Further, a multiple-source approach using observation, literature review, and interviews was chosen to analyze the issues.

5.2 THE WIDE FIELD OF EXPATRIATES

"For the contemporary expatriate, life is a process of mediating between physical and virtual realities. For the expatriate, even more than for the migrant moving from one location to another is not so much a transfer of self to new territory, as the repositioning of the physical body in another part of a web of visible and invisible connections. From most locations within this web, the same resources can be tapped, the same services used, the same entertainments enjoyed. The individuality of each location is arguably restricted to a layer of physical stimuli weather, local language, cuisine – that can be enjoyed, mediated or even virtually negated by globalized infrastructure." (Beynon 2008: 12)

This quote shows the flexibility with which urban citizens are already adapting to the increasingly temporary international people who come to town for work. It is a common assumption that an expatriate is only in China for a limited time. The global expatriate's key characteristics are globalized taste, which Beynon describes as "the Wallpaper modern style" (Beynon 2008:12) and the absence of traditional ties of belonging. As individuals, expatriates regularly transcend local and global borders as essential and committed participants in the globalized system of circulating capital, goods, and knowledge. Expatriates in China often use a globalized infrastructure without the need to become more integrated in the Chinese local culture, or to take a deeper interest in the new surroundings. In the context of this book we contemplate what it means to be a flexible expat and what it means to be excluded as privileged in the receiving society.

Figure 17: Resident Foreigners in Shanghai by Types

2009

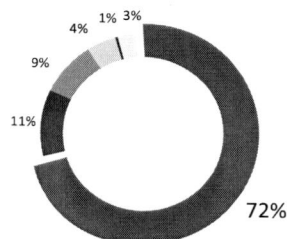

2013

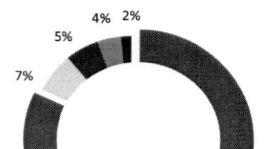

- 1. Employees and Relatives at Foreign Ventures
- 2. Overseas Students and Relatives
- 3. Delegate and Relatives of Institutions Stationed in China
- 4. Foreign Experts and Relatives
- 5. Permanent Resident Foreigners
  6. Long-term Vise Foreigners Above Half Year

- 1. Employees and Relatives at Foreign Ventures
- 2. Foreign Experts and Relatives
- 3. Overseas Students and Relatives
- 4. Delegate and Relatives of Institutions Stationed in China
- 5. Permanent Resident Foreigners

Source. Illustration Bronner | Reikersdorfer, based on Shanghai Statistical Yearbook 2009 and 2014

It turns out to be a great challenge to collect reliable data about foreigners in Shanghai as to their temporary nature. They are currently mainly reflected in business-oriented statistics like the HSBC expat explorer or Expatriates Aon Hewitt Assoiciates (2010)[4] for the Chinese market, which has been conducted annually since 2004. The study recognizes six categories of expats: those from the West; those from Hong Kong and Singapore; those from Taiwan; those from other Asian countries; foreigners who are employed by Chinese entities and hired in the Chinese market under local conditions and returnees. Expatriates

---

[4] Hewitt Associates conducted this survey in cooperation with the American Chamber of Commerce by British Chamber of Commerce, Chambre de Commerce et d'Industrie Française en Chine, China Australia Chamber of Commerce and the German Industry and Commerce.

hired directly from global corporate headquarters usually receive additional benefits including bonuses, housing, insurance, and education for their children, while almost all companies surveyed in 2011 did not give those benefits to locals, returnees, or foreigners with Chinese contracts. By 2015 however, this has slightly changed. High-level managing positions in foreign offices are more often filled by Chinese and returnees. Knowing their high value for the company, they often expect the benefits of expats (like housing allowance and payment of private education for their children) untypical for local contracts. Also there are more and more foreigners with Chinese contracts that include a certain expat benefit eg more vacation days or an annual flight home (Mercer 2014).

The expatriate package usually contains special conditions that employers offer to their employees when asking them to work abroad. If the company itself does not take care of the new arrivals, there are now countless companies, relocation services and chambers of commerce that provide these services. They have developed arrival packages to make the initial period of arrival to urban China as easy as possible. They provide support on various levels ranging from the consultancy for a market launch in China, finding the right accommodation, helping with visa applications, and offering legal support, to simple things like buying public transport tickets and organizing parties and events (ibid.). While most of these services classify expatriates as consumers, this book goes beyond the categorization of expatriates as objects for market research or recipients service packages.

Networks of Belonging

"Social relations do not disappear in the 'worldwide' framework. On the contrary, they are reproduced at that level. Via all kinds of interactions, the world market creates configurations and inscribes changing spaces on the surface of the earth, spaces governed by conflicts and contradictions." (Lefebvre 2009 [1974]: 404)

We are not surprised when we are told that people tend to stay close together when living abroad defined by ethnicity – Chinatown, Little Italy, the Latin Quarter, and the French Concession are typical names of such areas in global cities around the world (Saunders 2011). When newcomers create their own communities within the city, they tend not to intermingle with the local residents but rather stay close to people with a common background with whom they can speak their native language (Hofstede 2001 [1983]).

Expatriates in China from different cultural backgrounds often establish personal networks with different characteristics. Hofstede (2001 [1983]) has examined how different people behave and react in other cultures. He notes that we tend to make decisions based on our own value system, which contains the core elements of our culture of origin (ibid.); however, they are not always the right decisions for the new surroundings. We feel comfortable around people with similar values and behavior patterns, which partially explains the common phenomenon of urban residents clustering based on national origin and common language. However, the intent here is not to further highlight the cultural differences of such clusters in Shanghai, but rather to note the existence of large English, French, Spanish, German, and Dutch speaking communities. Although most expatriates are well connected to the rest of the world and their place of origin through mobile devices, they tend to exclude themselves from local communities. Hence, expatriates create familiar "networks of belonging" and seek connections between people, objects, memories, and associations (Beynon 2008:15). Throughout the years of foreign influence in Shanghai international association have been founded at the governmental, cultural, and university level, and additionally large Internet communities have recently emerged. A few examples serving to illustrate this point include The German Chamber of Commerce (AHK), the Goethe Institute Shanghai, the Royal Asiatic Society (RAS), The Shanghai Expatriate Association (SEA), and the American Club of Shanghai (ACS).

The following chapter includes observations of the contemporary spatial shift and the dynamics of urban change under foreign design influence in Shanghai.

Impacts on City Life

"Cities are mirrors of society and systems of governance of the country in which they are located." (Nowak in Burdett/Sudjic 2011: 6)

The socio-spatial transformation with influences by the West is reflected in Shanghai's cityscape. The status of cities is defined by the Chinese government in a tiered system that ranges from Tier 1 to Tier 3. The cities are not only classified by the number of inhabitants, but also by their economic and social importance. Beijing, Shanghai, and Guangzhou are Tier 1 cities and were one of the first cities to be opened up to competitive economic development in the early 1980s, which was followed by a tremendous increase in the number of foreigners. Until recently Tier 1 cities were more attractive for foreign direct investment by global companies, but there is a trend toward the development of a strong internal Chinese market in cities in the second, third, and fourth tiers (A.T

Kearney Index 2010). As a long term development goal the Chinese government intends to shift from a low-wage, export-oriented market to an internal market based on consumption (Schauhuber 2010: 107).

As a Tier 1 city Shanghai began to attract foreign investors back in the mid 1990s in four sectors: traditional manufacturing, high-tech manufacturing, financial services, and business headquarters. Shanghai's city administration opened Pudong New Area to foreign investment. The district, which is situated east of the Huangpu River, was "fed by the deregulation of financial markets, ascendance of finance and specialized services, and integration into the world markets" (Sassen 2001: 7) and offered special tax deals to attract foreign investment. The power of the market is reflected in the spatial development of Pudong as a central business district, "a place where the company headquarters of big business, banks, shopping centers, hotels, lately also cultural institutions and wealthy urbanites in fancy residential high-rise buildings assemble in order to add the symbolic capital of centrality to their image – and of course, vice versa" (Hassenpflug 2010: 68).

China's rapid economic race to catch up in the worldwide market manifests in an average Gross National Product (GDP) growth of ten percent per annum in recent years. To date an enormous amount of foreign capital (FDI) has been invested directly into the city's industrial and economic sectors and boosted the building industry (Li Xiangning/Zhang Xiachun 2008). The stimulated construction boom found spatial expression in Shanghai and nowadays one can find the new urban economic core of banking and service activities and a major office of almost every well-established national and international company in Pudong. With its astonishing and impressive skyline Pudong represents daily global business, but from the street level the perspective is different and it seems the design of the new city quarter didn't take the human scale into account.

Presently Shanghai is a key node in an increasingly networked global economy (Castells 1996 in Sassen 2001) and is shifting from a place of production to a center of producer services; this includes financial, legal, and management, innovation, development, design, administration, personnel, production technology, maintenance, transport, communications, wholesale distribution, advertising, cleaning, security, and storage services (Sassen 2001).

Reinforced by this transformation, there is an increasing need for expertise in various fields. Global cities like Shanghai have attracted an influx of highly skilled professionals (Sassen 2001; Findlay et al. 1995). It is evident that companies in highly competitive and innovative sectors with a strong world market orientation have a need for highly-educated foreign professional workers in Shanghai – as Sassen calls them knowledge workers.

Since 2010 Shanghai has been part of the UNESCO Creative Cities Network, which connects ideas and best practices for social and economic development. Shanghai is strongly promoting creative industries with a focus on design, improvement of the city's image and quality of life, enhancement of the social and economic benefits of the creative industries, and development of networks. Over time, the municipality has developed various beneficial strategies including strengthening the protection of intellectual property by implementing new laws and by promoting the renovation and reutilization of old urban areas and industrial buildings and transforming them to into creative clusters. Due to these factors Shanghai, with its fast growing market for design, was chosen as a strategic hub for the growing internal market.

Driven by economic development the government introduced trial measures allowing foreigners to purchase housing, first only in SEZs and, since 2001, also outside the SEZ Zones, as it became possible for foreigners to lease land use rights (Sommers/Philipps 2010). As a result over 100,000 foreigners, including non Mainland Chinese have purchased housing in Shanghai in the past few years, which has increased the demand on Western living standards (Li Xiangning/Zhang Xiachun 2008). Cities are and always have been nodes of global flows of capital, goods, and people. As Shanghai increasingly becomes a marketplace for global capital, increasing poverty, segregation, and continued marginalization of socially vulnerable groups follow. There have already been consequences of this increasing inequality: rising living costs combined with stagnant income levels have forced migrant workers to leave town and caused a labor shortage in the service industry. Due to the rapid pace and large scale of urban construction, Chinese cities will have a profound impact on the ecological health of the planet. One reason for China's current investment in renewable technologies for greater environmental equity is that it will facilitate cooperation with the West.

Impacts on Public Space Life

"China does not, at present, have a civil society in the contemporary Western sense. Its 'public sphere' has been absorbed by the party-state, and without it and the democratic institutions that make it possible, a civil society, such as Jürgen Habermas would have it, is inconceivable. China thus presents us with a paradox: an increasingly pluralist society within a monolithic political system." (Friedmann 2005: 12)

Following Friedmann's description of Chinese civil society, our approach to the subject of public space differs from the mainstream Western approach. Hassenpflug (2010:68) does not speak of a public sphere or public space in China; instead, he uses the term "open urban space". Gaubatz argues that on the one hand the physical landscape of Chinese cities has become more open and more public, but on the other hand Chinese urban space is increasingly filled with commercial spaces (Gaubatz 2008: 75). These usually expensive retail spaces are exclusive places that do not meet the daily needs of local residents. Critical urban theorists emphasize that "a public space is provided by the state and used by the society. [...] it is controlled by the public authorities, concerns people as a whole, is open or available to them, and is used or shared by all members of a community" (Madanipour 2003: 13).

The intention of providing a critical Western perspective on this subject is to draw attention to foreign influence in the redevelopment of urban open space, including the construction of new urban plazas and Western-style pedestrian areas. Today one can observe foreign influence in particular locations in Shanghai such as along the waterfront of the Huangpu River and Suzhou Creek, in Pudong as the new CBD, and also in the former foreign settlements such as the French Concession. Appadurai calls these places "translocalities", in which particular kinds of localities are created and sustained by the "continual presence of outsiders" (Appadurai 1996 in Beynon 2008: 192). Caused by an increasing demand on the part of the expatriate population for new drinking and dining establishments, many new designer bars and restaurants have opened in Shanghai, including the German Paulaner Brewery. A closer look at the transformation of open space currently occurring in China indicates that the rapid development of exclusive commercial space is leading to further segregation between local residents and expatriate communities.

5.3 Bubble Worlds – Spatial Conditions

Chinese urbanism in general and in Shanghai in particular is extremely rapid. It is not only economic and political changes that have led to this rapid urban development, but structural changes in society have also made the ongoing transformation of urban China possible. Post-reform urban development has been driven by increasingly opening policy, as well as the progression of the market economy on the one hand, and rising consumerism and individualism on the other (Davis 1995). In 1984 real estate enterprises began dealing with the urban housing market, which was previously regulated by the Chinese state. With the implementation of new reforms different income groups emerged and led to the rapid development of urban housing in the 1990s.

Until 1999 foreigners were required to live in residences such as hotel and hotel-style apartments, or in diplomatic areas, which had to be approved by the Public Security Bureau (cf. Freedom Hotel in Beijing in Gaubatz 2010). As part of the attempt to attract more foreign investment, Chinese authorities loosened the restrictions on housing for foreigners. The increase of the foreign population has led to increasing demand in the property sector and simultaneously to gentrification and the complete transformation of parts of the residential landscape (Wu/Webber 2004). The development of the so called *waixiao fang* (外销房 foreign housing market) was a response to the lack of high quality housing. In turn, this has led to the "concentration of expatriates' housing into foreign enclaves" (ibid).

Most expatriates used to receive salaries far greater than the average local income. Together with the Chinese new rich, they constituted a significant consumer group and are potential purchasers of the middle and high-end commercial residences that have been built since the 1990s (Li Xiangning/Zhang Xiaochun 2008). Generally speaking, the key feature of foreign residential housing is that it is more luxurious than domestic housing. To fulfil the requirements of this new consumer group, many foreign companies have entered the real estate market in order to meet and understand their clients' needs and demands in terms of architecture and design. As a result of changing policy and the expansion of the housing market a shift from an excluded to a consumer group can be observed. The term international community usually refers to neighbourhoods where 30 % of the population is foreign (ibid.). The communities are often located in downtown areas close to the workplace or at the fringe of the city close to an international school. Leach refers to this phenomenon as "living in an aesthetic cocoon" (Leach 2001: 104). It is an example of the globalized elite's reaction or desire to the exclusion of ordinary everyday life – a retraction into aestheticized comfort, a kind of generic high-style environment inhabited worldwide by "Wallpaper people" (ibid.:105).

The contemporary urban planning and residential housing design in China has been strongly affected by the Western architectural style broadcast by the media. "The market-orientated nature of the real estate market fulfills those created dreams of Chinese 'new rich' for a 'better life' with playful inclination towards symbolism" (Hassenpflug 2010: 61).

"The new rich […] began to seek difference and diversity; gated suburbia, tactically promoted by the real estate developer as an 'exotic' and 'stylish' new living space, meets such an imagination for a good life that gated communities are branded through a mélange of metaphors such as 'classic', 'continental', 'authentic'. 'European' and 'North American' lives, have indeed become the de-contextualied and diverse built forms." (Wu Fulong, 2006 in Hassenpflug 2010: 63)

In China gated communities were created due to a gap between the demand for such housing and the available supply, which was restricted by institutional constraints. They serve as a striking example of foreign influence on China's transforming residential landscape (Wu/Webber 2004). A gated community is a housing development that "restricts public access through the use of gates, fences, walls" (Atkinson/Blandly 2005: 178). In urban China gated housing also existed in the tradition of work unit compounds. Wu Fulong further compares work-unit compounds to housing enclaves, noting that the gate itself has existed in China for a long time, but is now being "rediscovered as an instrument to control space and represents a complex tension between community of shared lifestyles and values to enhance social interaction and further excludes non-members from interaction" (ibid.: 249). Nowadays the link between workplace and living as it existed in the *danweis* environment is becoming less common. They are being replaced by housing developments.

Currently the gate represents the entrance to commodified residential urban space. Here, "a space of differentiation gives a new function to the 'gate' of excluding people of lower socio-economic status" and leads to residential segregation (Wu Fulong 2005: 241). There are two trends in the development of high-end residences in Shanghai: high-rise apartment complexes – better known as compounds – and low-rise villa compounds with private gardens further away from the dense city core. Both dwelling forms are gated communities, which according to Richard Sennett (2008) define and enshrine boundaries of social, economic, religious, and ethnic groups and create static territories in the cities of the twentieth century.

When looking at the Chinese residential housing industry, we focus on the current living conditions of expatriates, who tend to concentrate in clusters in Shanghai. The available services, the high quality of the buildings, and the exclusiveness of living make it attractive for foreigners to live in gated communities; even though foreigners are now officially allowed to settle in any residence, expatriates often prefer to live inside these isolated environments. "Foreign housing is characterized by luxurious design standards, high rent, high security, a clean living environment, and a large variety of facilities [...] such as swimming pool, tennis court, restaurant and landscaped gardens [...]" (Wu/Webber 2004: 208). Additionally, international hospitals and medical centres, shopping centres, and Western supermarkets are often situated near foreigners' compounds. Today, foreign enclaves have become a synonym for high-quality living and represent "fully commodified housing" that has its roots in China's economic transition (ibid.: 209). Even though most foreigners are accustomed to different dwelling forms in their home countries, they tend to live in gated communities in China, as do a rising number of local residents. Additionally, linguistic and cultural barriers and the fact that they are often only temporarily in town make it difficult for them to establish friendships and relationships with local residents.

Soon after the foreign housing market was created, it was entered by domestic buyers who were attracted to the high quality of buildings and the associated high living standard. In traditional Chinese neighbourhoods the social structure is very tight and often restrictive. Hence, there is great appeal in the type of life that these anonymous gated residences offer: "purified – only living qualities with no social expectation combined" (Wu Fulong 2005: 245). Thus, caused by the enormous growth of gated communities, Shanghai's residential landscape has increasingly become characterized by spatial and social fragmentation. This in turn prevents the unique mixture of meaningful city lives.

When analyzing foreign housing in China it becomes evident that various unsolved issues remain concerning the living conditions of foreigners. We are making a two-pronged argument: on the one hand it is foreign residents' own intention to be separated and excluded from everyday life; on the other hand there are few attractive alternatives.

5.4 Working Challenges

"Throughout the city, whole blocks are being flattened, turning parts of the former 'Paris of the East' into huge construction sites – a chorus of cranes, jack-hammers and bulldozers chiseling out the foundations of skyscrapers, elevated expressways and subway tunnels. Architects are having their fling with modernism – designing huge glass-faced offices complexes and luxury apartment blocks." (Yatsko in Fulong Wu/Xu Jiang/Yeh 2007: 2)

Within the vast population of expatriates we are particular interested in the role of Western architects and planners. The following chapter includes our observations of foreign architects and their place in the contemporary construction industry in China with its profit making building practices. These observations are complemented by a focus on the adoption of Western designs by Chinese developers and the relationship between the Chinese and foreign parties in the process of planning, preparation, and construction. Hence different views of foreign planners, Chinese real estate developers, and Chinese design partners (Local Design Institute – LDI) are presented for a better understanding of the complex process.

"Every major Chinese city today has its flashy, foreign-designed building – form Guangzhou's much admired opera house to the striking new headquarters of China Central Television in Beijing." (Miller 2012: 139)

Due to China's huge number of exports and its booming real estate market, it is predicted that there will be a simultaneous and growing demand for new infrastructure and living space. As a result, the Chinese government has been investing in building a huge amount of physical infrastructure for much of the past three decades (Zakaria 2010). Amounts in excess of hundreds of billions of *renminbi* have been released for infrastructure projects, which range from roads, bridges to new railway lines. In order to meet the enormous demand for new building projects and to prevent construction errors caused by a lack of knowledge, China has been hiring foreign design companies to contribute their designs and ideas for the undeveloped land. The rapid urban development in the first years of the new millennium represented an attractive opportunity for Western planners to come to China to be part of the "gold rush" (Lu Xin 2008: 23). Chinese cities have become significant objects of interest for Western architects, planners, and urban scholars who are fascinated by and curious about the speed of urban transformation.

The drive toward modernization has caused rapid economic development followed by rapid urbanization, and the Shanghai Planning Bureau has officially called for introducing advanced planning concepts from foreign countries in 2001. This led to a large expat community in the field of architecture, design, and engineering. Also, Shanghai has been influenced by architecture designed by foreigners. No other nation has experienced the construction of such a large quantity of foreign architectural designs over such a short period of time (Xue/Zhou 2007). Due to the current slow-down in the construction sector, architectural offices tend to hire experienced architects in the Chinese market with a crucial understanding of the Chinese culture and language (EU SME 2015).

In 2004 Rem Koolhaas called upon Western architects to GO EAST to participate in China's urbanization process. In his publication Content (2004) he offers "an attempt to illustrate the architect's ambiguous relations with the forces of globalization, an account of seven years spent scouring the earth – not as business traveler or backpacker, but as vagabond – roving, searching for an opportunity to realize the visions that make remaining at home torturous"

(McGetick in Koolhaas 2004: 16). Up to date many internationally renowned architectural offices are also involved in the Chinese construction boom commissioned to design iconic architecture. The power of architecture as symbol has roots in the Chinese hierarchical structure of society, in which architecture demonstrates status (Hassenpflug 2010). The Shanghai Tower, designed by the architectural firm Gensler, is extreme in scale and ambition at 632 meters high. Qingwei Kong, the President of the Shanghai Tower Construction & Development Co, Ltd. describes the building as "symbolic of a nation whose future is filled with limitless opportunities" (Gensler 2011). Despite the strong tradition of symbolism in Chinese architecture, the directive recently issued by the State Council, China's cabinet and the Communist Party's Central Committee says 'no' to any architecture considered 'oversized' or 'weird' (Cao Li 2016) Influences on the implementation remain to be seen.

Not only iconic architecture, but also copies of Western style architecture became an increasing demand of Chinese clients. Today, these influences from the West are clearly visible in China. Some of them are rendered in concrete and have a direct effect upon urban life. Shanghai's 'One City, Nine Villages' satellite city plan was largely designed by Western architects, who created these villages using several European cities as models. The urban planning and design reflects Chinese enthusiasm towards Western design on a profound and unprecedented scale (cf. Hassenpflug 2010). The huge built areas are a reproduction of typical American, British, Dutch, German, Italian, Spanish, and Swedish architectural styles. It could be inferred that China is becoming "westernized", which could mean that the country is losing its identity (Lu Xin 2008).

However, we should be cautious when speaking of the westernization of China. First, the concept of westernization should be distinguished from the concept of globalization. On the one hand globalization is a worldwide phenomenon and takes many forms, including the globalization of economic, capital, design, technology, and education; on the other hand the term westernization refers to the process by which societies are influenced by or adopt Western culture in industry, technology, law, politics, economics, lifestyle, design, and architecture (Lu Xin 2008: 26). At the same time we should consider the acculturation process that foreign architects undergo when they enter the new, foreign working environment. They remain strongly influenced by their native culture – their enculturation code – and it seems logical that these architects would work and act according to Western code of professional ethics.

"The role of a designer is very important. With knowledge of materials, the needs of the people, the cost of construction, he looks for the quality of a space. And when beauty comes, then the architect sings." (Nguyen Chi Tam in Sinclair 2007)

Working in China is challenging but also offers nearly infinite opportunities for skilled Western professional planners. Based on interviews, personal experience, and scholarly literature we provide an overview of the different tasks in which these foreign experts are involved during the design and construction process. From the planner's perspective the large scale of projects in China presents unique and unprecedented opportunities. The large scales of the projects are not only reflected in their size, but also in capital and resources required. This leads to particular obligations and expectations that the planning parties must fulfill. High pressure brought on by a large amount of work and the imperative of meeting deadlines is a side effect of the competitive working environment found in the profit-oriented construction industry. Due to different conditions and regulations as well as the cross-cultural working environment, it can be a challenge for Western architects to maintain an awareness of the big picture at all times (Lu Xin 2008).

Ongoing differences, misunderstandings, and disputes are common during architectural practice worldwide, but foreign planners face additional challenges that are even more complex than those they face at home. The differences between Eastern and Western planning approaches have been a major topic of discussion among architects in recent years. Xin Lu (2008) describes the different design approaches and offers general insight as to how these influence the evolving process of construction. Based on her research, Western architects tend to spend more time at the beginning of the construction process analyzing the given situation, setting up a functional layout, and developing a design according to defined design parameters. This contrasts with Chinese architects, who come up with design proposals very quickly (ibid.). Regardless of which approach towards planning or design one was taught in architecture school – rational and flexible; site specific, contextual and culturally sensitive – it is not clear whether those trained in the West are properly prepared for the major challenge of coming to work in China.

In 'Criticality in between China and the West' Zhu Jianfei (2005) further emphasizes the point that these different approaches to architectural design are significant. He argues that critical thinking and the mechanisms needed to produce a critical discourse have a long tradition in Europe and can be traced back to the enlightenment: "that condition of being which speaks of the possibility in being of knowledge" (Eisenman in Zhu Jianfei 2005: 480). According to Zhu the

Western separation between theory and practice is not suitable for China. Further, he calls for more research to explore "communication as intersection in-between the cultures" in order to develop a more critical understanding of this phenomenon (Zhu Jianfei 2005: 496).

The Chinese tendency of referring to traditions and culture is remarkable when compared to other post-socialist countries. Traditional concepts are still given great importance in Chinese society, and most architects find that they need to take them into account during planning stages (Hassenpflug 2010). One example is *feng shui* (风水), the Chinese concept of harmony of space based on *yin* and *yang* (阴阳). A well know example of the importance of *feng shui* is when Sir Norman Foster was compelled to adjust the angle of the escalators in the lobby of his HSBC building in Hong Kong to be harmonious with *feng shui* principles, even though this change may have seemed unreasonable from a Western architect's point of view (ibid.: 39).

By drawing attention to the cultural traditions of European architectural practice based in the Arts and Crafts movement (e.g. Bauhaus), we complement our discussion of cultural differences in planning approaches. Furthermore, in the case of China we have found that production forces and design forces are not closely linked in architecture. Ideally, an effective dialogue can emerge through mutual understanding: the designer can incorporate an understanding of the processes of production and the manufacturer can incorporate an understanding of design processes into their work. This shows the importance of developing a closer relationship between East and West, theory and practice, planning and implementation.

For the vast majority of architectural firms, establishing an independent architecture office proves to be quite complicated. According to Li Na, a specialist on legal issues faced by foreign architecture, planning, and design offices, foreign architecture firms have three options. They can either directly collaborate with a Chinese architecture institute (local design institute – LDI), set up an architecture enterprise in China (Foreign Institute Enterprise – FIE) or establish a wholly foreign-owned consulting enterprise (WFOE) (Li Na 2007). Foreign-founded architectural companies in China are especially established for the Chinese market with a foreign architect as founder or co-founder. The common practice of collaboration limits the activities of foreign offices to preliminary design and further consultancy, which means they hand over responsibility to the LDI after completing the design phase. The mainly state owned LDIs have expertise on Chinese national building regulations and are responsible for the implementation phases of construction. This cooperative model often creates tensions between the various planning parties, as the LDI holds the required licenses and permits for construction. The Chinese partner organizations keep a tight hold on construction documents, the construction and the supervision. In order to successfully conduct business in China as a foreign architectural office it is crucial to maintain a good relationship and close contact with the Chinese client. In the course of the building process it is the investor's responsibility to determine whether or not the focus of the project is on design, quality, and sustainability.

As there are so many different stakeholders in the construction process, incorrect interpretation of the design, poor quality of implementation, and ineffective or insufficient communication can generate conflicts during the realization of the project. The result often does not meet the expectations of foreign designers, and frustration is common. There can be many reasons: firstly, the legal framework and conditions surrounding intellectual property rights are not enforced. Secondly, it has become increasingly common that design services are not paid according to the contract (Winkler 2011). Other architects see it simply as an issue of principle to not become involved in construction in China. They see it as working for a country that lacks effective laws that protect individuals and their civil rights (Amnesty International Report 2010). Architects who do build in China are sometimes criticized by Western colleagues and media. One well-known example of this is the so called "bird's nest" project, the stadium for the Olympics Games in 2008 by Swiss architects Herzog & de Meuron, who were criticized after the inhumane working conditions to meet completion dates were revealed (Schaub/Schindhelm 2008). Even though foreign architecture offices are highly visible in the creative sector and in architectural media, their responsibilities and share in the Chinese market are limited (Muynck 2009).

Summary – Global Urban Nomads

When observing global urban nomads in detail we were able to acquire scientific knowledge about this specific group. Certain findings helped us to gain greater intellectual insight and it became clear that the phenomena discussed have multiple causes, which led to multiple ways to gain deeper insight. The observed mosaic of life-worlds is complex.

Social Networks
A network of internationally connected people living in Shanghai has organized an infrastructure tailored to suit arriving foreigners; thus, when expats come to Shanghai they are greeted with numerous offers upon arrival including survival packages and support services. These support services on arrival are manifold but also have their cost; the more extensive the offer, the more expensive it is.

Expats have been recognized as a target group with strong purchasing power, and their new demands have strongly influenced supply. The reasons why foreigners have been recognized as a consumer group in Shanghai are largely tied to historic events. Regulated by law, they have been concentrated in communities within Special Economic Zones.

Spatial Conditions

The Chinese urban housing market began to integrate the needs and demands of consumers and paid more attention to comfort and higher living standards. At the same time the freedom of choice in housing led to the differentiation, reconfiguration, and segregation of urban space. As a result, post-Mao economic reforms have led to dramatic changes in the relationships between space, time, state, and society. This dynamic urbanization can be seen not only in physically perceivable urban space, but also in the fast-paced working and living conditions to which the inhabitants are subjected. With demand being closely linked to capital, they have also influenced the supply of space in the city, which has led to a transformation of the residential landscape. The foreign housing market is characterized by an apartment design imported from the West and adapted to the new requirements of living in Shanghai, but as a result this cocooned living has led to further segregation between local residents and the expatriate communities. This can be seen in the city wherever foreigners have been defined as a consumer group, influencing commercial retail spaces and other commercialized open spaces.

Working Challenges

Also historically determined was the need for modernization in China's cities after Mao had prevented city development for three decades. The current building boom in China's cities that has attracted such great numbers of foreign architects has resulted in an extremely rapid pace of development. In spite of this spatial development, Western architects are often not up to the challenges they face, due to unfamiliar aspects of the foreign culture and a completely new scale and context of architectural production. We have observed that, in the course of adapting to the new working environment, architects often remain silent or uninterested when dealing with situations where working and living conditions of other participants in the construction process clearly do not meet international standards of safety and decency.

6. Rural Urban Nomads

没有比临时移民更永久的。
Méiyǒu bǐ línshí yímín gèng yǒngjiǔ de.
"There is nothing as permanent as a temporary migrant"
CHINESE SAYING

Figure 18: The Number of Rural Migrant Workers in Various Years

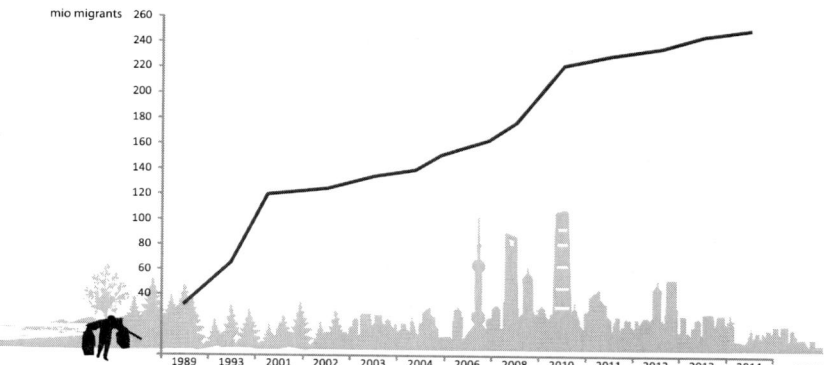

Source. Illustration Bronner | Reikersdorfer, based on Chinese National Bureau of Statistics, 2009 and 2014

In China the term *dagong* is used to describe the phenomenon of labour migration quite accurately – literally being employed – and stands especially for rural people seeking work elsewhere and for people working in temporary or casual jobs. Rural migrant workers are a particular group resulting from China's economic transition. They are called *nongmingong* (农民工) – peasants who have become migrant workers. While the previous section discussed global business migrants, this part focuses on rural migrant construction workers. In order to understand the various causes that led to rural working migrants' living and working conditions, it is helpful to take a closer look at their present situation. First, we will analyse the working conditions of rural migrant construction workers and by doing so highlight the individuals and their ways of life. Secondly, we will investigate their immediate surroundings and living conditions. To contextualize these conditions, the third part will provide an overview of the relevant political, legal, and social situation, which highly influences the lives of rural migrant workers in the city. This includes their social status within Chinese society, which is affected by the *hukou* system, as well as the effect of organizations with different strategies to help migrant workers.

6.1 Approaching from Outside

The use of different approaches was essential for us in order to gain a broader understanding of the group under investigation. The following description is based largely on interviews, and construction site visits. To collect and structure these information we kept a research diary. The fieldwork took place at several construction sites in Shanghai and its urban fringe. Access to these sites was mainly obtained through a project management company that allowed us to conduct interviews with all parties on the construction site. The life stories and interviews were collected with the help of a Chinese architect who introduced us to our respondents and who also partially translated some of the more complex interviews, such as those with construction site managers, when our own Chinese skills weren't sufficient or when interview partners spoke dialects other than Mandarin. Without their kind support the interviews could not have taken place. Because we were able to access additional sites in Kunshan and Taicang, both towns on Shanghai's urban fringe, we included these as well.

By choosing our respondents from a wide variety of fields within the construction industry, we were able to include a broad variety of perspectives on our research topic. It was necessary for us to have several conversations with workers, subcontractors, planners, and project managers in order to understand the complex circumstances of migrant workers on construction sites in China. We were also able to adopt different roles as part of the process. While we were part of the research group in the case study of global urban nomads, our research on rural urban nomads was conducted from the outside. This gave us the chance to recognize problems that the respondents are not conscious of because they are accustomed to the siutation. On the other hand, the subjects obviously know more about their circumstances than anyone else. We pursued an approach that combines bottom-up research methods and personal narratives as a powerful means to link migrants to qualitative survey field data and the literature. We have used pseudonyms to protect their privacy.

During our research the construction workers interviewed often asked us even more questions than we asked them. They were very curious about our background, about construction sites in Europe, and about wages and the price of construction materials. For almost every question we asked them, they wanted to know the answer as it pertained to Austria. Thus, many interviews were in essence an intercultural exchange enjoyed by both parties, who were both asking and responding to questions. While this qualitative approach does not claim to gain representative findings, it is from our perspective more important to identify processes, illuminates structures, and understand how different perspectives intersect. In addition to the interviews, a multiple-source approach using observation and document analysis was applied to contextualize the case study to our research framework. Through several snapshots we combine individual histories with an overview of the bigger picture of socio-spatial transformations in Shanghai.

6.2 WORKING CONDITIONS ON SITE

The construction industry in China is dominated by a multi-layered system of contracts and subcontracts. Usually, about 15-20 people from the same family, neighbourhood, or village organize themselves as a work group under one group leader (*daigong*) and are contracted for one project by a subcontractor (*baogongtou*), who works for a contractor (*dabao*) employed by a (usually state-owned) construction company. As one of the interviews in Kunshan revealed, many migrant workers are hired directly by small private companies, or find their job through a contractor, usually someone the migrant workers know from their hometown or are related to. This shows that workers depend on their social network when searching for work. A direct employer is absent due to the many layers of contractors and subcontractors. Once a group is formed and has a contract with a *baogongtou*, the group members begin the often very long journey directly to the urban building site.

Figure 19: Subcontracting System on a Chinese Construction Site

PROPERTY DEVELOPER

CONSTRUCTION COMPANY - mainly state-owned

CONTRACTOR (dabao) - provides raw materials

SUBCONTRACTOR (baogongtou) - manages daily workassignments

WORKGROUP organized by one (daigong) - 15 to 20 people usually from the same village
Source. Illustration Bronner | Reikersdorfer, based on Chinese National Bureau of Statistics, 2009 and 2014

"All the way he was looking forward to the beautiful life there and not in his dreams he thought that the city could be so different. When he arrived on the construction site, he was disappointed immediately. The living conditions were truly very bad. [...] Dajun should now learn thoroughly what it means to live in a prison." (Lu Huilin in Pun Ngai 2010: 25)[5]

Pun Ngai (2010) describes scenarios of departure and journeys of construction workers leaving their hometowns to work in the city. This excitement often lasts only until the migrants arrive at their workplace, as Dajun's story shows. Comparing a construction site and a prison might seem severe, but this image appears repeatedly in literature, songs, and interviews. Examples include *"Wǒ shì yī zhǐ xiǎo xiǎo niǎo"* (我是一只小小鸟 ; I am just a little bird, by Zhao Chuan) and *"Working Is Our Glory and Our Hell"*, which features lyrics like "[...] we are doomed and there is no escape [...]". These are well known songs among migrant workers.

Migrant workers almost never leave the construction site during a work assignment because they not only work but also live there. "Basically, nobody ever leaves the work site, because what money do we have to spend? Except for buying laundry detergent, shoes, and gloves, there's no reason to leave [the work site]" (construction worker in Human Rights Watch 2008: 30). Thus, the construction site is the centre of daily life for construction workers and serves as a

---

5   Own translation.

central node for street vendors offering everything from food to other day-to-day necessities. Living and working at the same place results in dependencies on the employer that have very strong impact on personal lives of workers.

The majority of rural migrant workers are engaged in low-end occupations, due in part to limited education and also to discrimination in the urban labour market (cf. Fan 2008; Awe 2007; Murphy 2009; Nielsen 2008). At the current practice, there are no particular educational requirements to be hired on a construction site. The largest proportion of construction workers have graduated from lower-middle school and have had no further education than this compulsory schooling. Around 70% of migrant workers are between 20 and 40 years old[6] and their only training is learning by doing *(bian zuò bian xué)*. This low educational attainment is why they are usually referred to as low-skilled rural migrant workers.

Figure 20: Distribution of Rural Migrant Workers by Educational Attainment, 2010

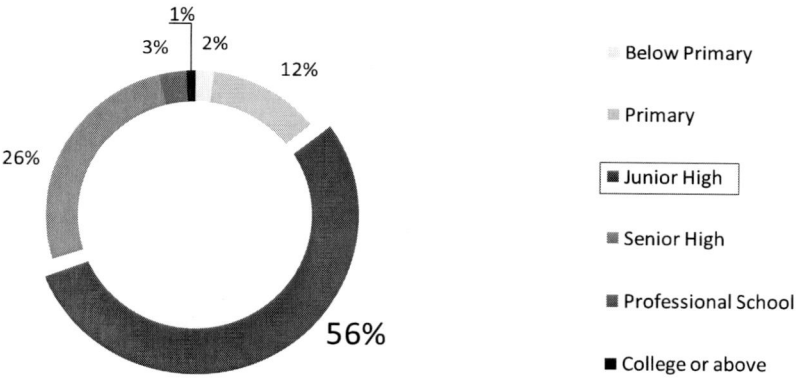

Source. Illustration Bronner | Reikersdorfer, based on Rual-Urban Migrant Survey in China Perspectives 2010.

Migrant construction workers' tasks usually consist of non-specialized, hard physical labour during the entire construction process. Most jobs in the construction sector are "intense, dangerous, and harsh and are therefore not attractive to

---

6 According to RUMS 2007 in China Perspectives 2010/4 which investigated 5,000 migrant households in 15 cities from 9 provinces.

local urban residents" (Shi Li 2010: 11). They are also often referred to as "3-D jobs: dirty, dangerous, and demanding" (Awe 2007:11).

Figure 21: Main Industries of Migrant Workers, 2007 and 2014

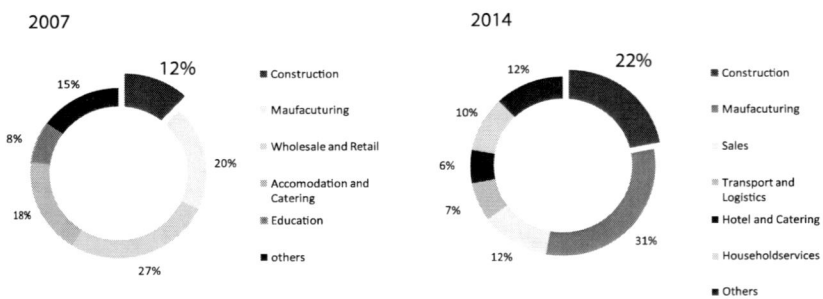

Source. Illustration Bronner I Reikersdorfer, based on Rural-Urban Migrant Survey conducted by the Project of China Rural Migration in China Perspectives, 2010 and China Labour Bulletin, 2016.

Observations by one of the workers interviews in Taicang showed, that low-skilled rural construction workers in China have oral agreements with their contractor about pay, working hours, and work tasks. They are not part of the official system and compliance with the terms and conditions of employment depend on the reliability of the subcontractor. If the contract conditions are not met on the part of the employer, it is nearly impossible for the workers to make any claims due to the lack of a written contract and official paperwork. Therefore, workers rely heavily on the relationships they have with their boss and currently there is no way to be sure of payment other than to trust that the employer will pay the full wages owed. With working conditions such as these, workers are always at risk of being deceived (Pun Ngai/Ching Kwan Lee 2010). The majority of migrant workers in all industries face problems of lack of job security and of exploitation. In 2004, 87.5 percent had non-signed labour contracts according to a survey conducted by the Ministry of Labour and Social Security (Shi Li 2010:14). Even though China's new Labour Contract Law was released in 2008, the rate of no written paper contracts in the construction industry remained at 74 percent (Li Yuwen 2011).

Another complexity of oral contracts is that rural migrant workers are not affiliated with the company they work for. High employee turnover is typical for companies in various sectors in China, and this is particularly true in the unskilled labour market, where workers have very high mobility as a result of strong competition and the lack of information on the real conditions of migrant worker jobs (Wemheuer 2011). This high mobility is also used as an instrument against the ongoing exploitation of workers (Pun Ngai/Kwan Lee 2010). Construction site managers often delay payment as a means of holding on to workers who might otherwise leave. However, when former workers were asked in a survey why they left their job, 41 percent chose low pay, 15 percent instability of the job, and 8 percent bad working conditions (Shi Li 2010). To prevent such a high turnover on the construction site, workers are sometimes required to leave a deposit of 3-4 months' salary with the employer. In many cases, they only receive their wages once a year: before they go home for Chinese New Year.

Long working hours are one of the characteristics of rural migrant jobs in all fields. Over 80 percent of rural migrants worked seven days per week as shown in the 2002 China Household Income Project Survey (CHIPS)[7] data, and for every day that is not worked, wages will not be earned. One of the interviewers in Kunshan pointed out on a regular schedule and the consequences of not finishing his task: A typical work week has seven work days, and only bad weather conditions are a reason to take a day off. Average working hours on the construction site are from 6:00 am to 5:00 pm with breakfast at 5:30 am, a one hour lunch break at 11:00 am, and dinner after 5:00 pm. Even though the work is very tiring, migrants work more than 10 hours per day. The group leader (*daigong*) is required to finish a particular task with his group on an almost daily basis, e.g., a particular number of steel beams or m² of concrete. If the task is not completed, work is continued after dinner or the subcontractor (*baogongtou*) refuses to pay that day's wages (Interview Mr. Chen 2010). This is why workers say of their contractors: "*tianxia wuya yiban hei* – all crows are black under the sky"[8] when referring to the many impossible work orders they had received from the subcontractor (*baogongtou*) at different construction sites.

"Take this building I am working on as an example, it's named Phoenix Island Health Resort, I heard it will cost 80,000 yuan per square meter. How wonderful would it be if I can let my mother come and live here? [...] But my monthly salary is 1,600 yuan, if I don't eat anything and just work, in about 5 years I can buy 1 square meter." (A young migrant worker, ChinaHush November 29th, 2009)

---

7   CHIPS, 2002, in China Perspectives 2010/4. The survey investigated 2,000 rural-urban migrant households in 12 provinces.
8   *tianxia wuya yiban hei* (天下乌鸦一般黑) by Cao Xueqin "Dream of the Red Chamber" in "Aufbruch der 2. Generation".

Data from China Labour Bulletin indicates that the average monthly wage in 2014 was 3,292 yuan[9], therefore the construction sector is among the highest-paid sectors for migrant workers. Although the income for construction workers has increased in the last years, the low income and security in payment is still a major problem. In 1994 minimum wages were defined in the Labour Law for the first time, but these are often not met by the employers (CLB 2011). Salaries are often held back for several months and 1.4 percent of the migrant construction workers in 2014 experienced wage arrears (CLB 2015). Usually the cost of board and lodging is deducted from the salary, with the daily rate varying from RMB 4 to RMB 10 (Interviews 2010). Based on an interview in Kunshan the average daily wage of migrant construction workers depends on their experience. In 2010 there were three wage levels ranging from RMB 80 for unskilled workers, RMB 120 for skilled workers, and RMB 160 for specialist workers.

"Why are migrant workers in the pictures wearing white hats and red hats, no one is wearing the normal yellow hat? Yellow hats are for leaders, they are from the construction company. They get monthly salary and we are paid by the hours, work one day and get paid for one day. If we get a cold, then there will be no pay. However the yellow hats are not bad people. Manager Yang wears a yellow hat, he goes to work earlier than us, and is the last person leaving the site. He hasn't gone home for 2 years already. He is the quality responsible person at the construction site. One day, I saw him crying by himself, I knew he also misses home!" (A young construction migrant worker, China Hush 2009)

Historically provided by the *danwei* workers' unit, job insurance, pensions, unemployment insurance, medical insurance, and public housing subsidies are now expected to be covered by the employer. However, rural migrant workers who are not registered with their *hukou* at their temporary residence are not entitled to the same social security benefits that local urban workers are. According to the National Bureau of Statistics (2010), nearly 75 percent of rural migrant workers were not covered by any insurance, although since July 2010 there is a law requiring health insurance for all workers and salaried employees (CLB 2011). And while employment conditions in many cases are rather harsh, the lack of protection leads to another form of discrimination against rural migrant workers. There are ways to participate in insurance programs, but a general distrust keeps them from paying for health insurance on their own initiative (Fan 2008). Thus

---

9   In 2016 RMB 3,292 converts to approximately 462 EUR, based on the January 2016 exchange rate RMB 1,000 is worth EUR 140.

more than two-thirds of migrant workers do not go to the hospital when needed due to cost (HDR China 2008). They also often struggle with their insurance due to changes in Chinese health-care financing in each region and usually, coverage cannot be transferred to a new region; many workers thus do not want insurance that is bound to one area.

6.3 SPATIAL CONFIGURATIONS

Construction workers tend to live in prefabricated housing situated next to the building site, ad hoc housing that is usually provided by the employer (Wang Ya Ping/Wan Yanglin 2009). Sometimes migrants even live in basements of just-completed high-rises or building shells on site. Empty rooms in factories and warehouses are also used for accommodation. If migrant workers do not live on site they usually find accommodation in the periphery of the city, as there are no sufficient or affordable private rentals in the city. These villages on the urban fringe are called *chengzhongcun* (urban villages), and the arrival of *waidiren* (outsiders) often disrupts the traditional society in these places, which is characterised by family ties (Wang Ya Ping/Wan Yanglin/Wu Jiansheng 2007). Migrants are often excluded from any decision making, which leads to a fragmentation of social space in the urban village. Even if migrant workers stay at in these places for years they do not become a part of the community and are treated as sojourners. Rural migrant workers usually also have their own property in their hometown, where the left-behind family lives.

In the construction sector it is very common for several workers or families of the workers to share a room. A joint project by researchers from Heriot-Watt University and Beijing University that surveyed about 800 migrant households shows that "those who share rooms with other families or individuals have the lowest standard of living. On average four persons share a room with an average floor space of only 7.7 square meters per person. In some instances over twenty people share a room, and some individuals have only 2 or 3 square meters of living space" (ibid.: 16). It becomes obvious that the living space of migrant workers is very limited and offers little privacy. The construction site shelters we observed during our research in and around Shanghai had several one- or two story dormitory buildings, one commonly used bathhouse, and a canteen. The prefabricated houses consisted of several rooms, each room housing up to six people. The only individual area inside the dormitory was the bunk beds. The essentials such as water, electricity, and sanitary facilities were insufficient.

Field Research

Figure 22: Construction Workers in Kunshan

Source. Bronner | Reikersdorfer 2011

They had been working all day, setting up the container houses piece by piece. Prefabricated panels, steel frames, and a few screws to put everything together. Every second panel includes a window, every third panel is a door, and while a long row of panel-window-door-panel-window-door is assembled, the future residents might not have been assigned yet. Opposite the buildings being constructed are two brick houses with a water source; a few missing bricks let light into the rooms. At the moment these rooms are used for sleeping by the assembling team, but as soon as the prefabricated homes are finished and the designated tenants arrive, the brick hall will be used as *shitang* (食堂 , canteen) and the other

brick areas as bathrooms. Each container room will be furnished with two three-level bunk beds for the numerous construction workers who will be living here while building a new project. And while the construction team is settling down for the next two or three years, the assembling team will move to the next building site to set up more housing for construction workers.
(Research Notes, November 2010)

Figure 23: Prefabricated Houses in Kunshan

dorms *sushi* canteen *shitang*
Source. Bronner | Reikersdorfer 2011

Some of the interviews for this book took place at a construction site in Kunshan where building was just about to start. Six workers from Jiangsu province were busy setting up prefabricated dorms and three workers from Anhui province were bringing up the walls for the canteen and bathhouse. Around 60 workers were expected to arrive in the days to come to erect a production building for a factory with 8000m² GFA. The workers were expected to arrive in small groups of 15-20 people and would then be responsible for different areas and subsections during the construction process. The houses were similar to containers and were made of prefabricated elements. The rooms looked like train berths, each fitting two bunks with three stacked beds each. According to a subcontractor the workers were expected to live on this site for approximately two years, before moving on to the next site.

The provided prefabricated shelters are typically constructed primarily of fireproof polystyrene sandwich panels and are supported with steel construction scaffolding. These panels serve as both walls and roof and are poor insulators. They are mounted between cold rolled c-beams, leaving only openings for one door and one window in each room. The roof usually consists of sandwich panels combined with corrugated metal sheets, which can be either single or double sloped. The lifespan of these prefabricated buildings is estimated at 20 years, which means that, if the average project lasts two years, they could house ten cycles of migrant workers. For each cycle they are dismantled and rebuilt on different construction sites.

This prefabricated standardized design supposedly satisfies the basic need for shelter; but when compared to other urban dwellings or the original living conditions of workers in their home villages, it becomes clear that this is substandard housing. Overall, migrant workers suffer from extremely difficult living and working conditions. They live either directly at their work sites or in low-quality housing concentrated at the urban fringe. Far away from their homes and families, they live a permanently temporary existence. There is now consensus among researchers that the quality of housing for migrants is below common standard of acceptable housing and that many rural migrants are living in absolute poverty (CLB 2011; Fan 2008; Jacka 2005; Murphy 2009). Moreover, mass accommodation and living on site allows maximum control and surveillance by the employer.

The living conditions of migrant construction workers are far from the adequate, dignified shelters as mentioned in the UN document for Human Rights. Article 25 of the Universal Declaration of Human Rights states that adequate housing is a fundamental human right (UN 1948). The Prefabricated dwellings on construction sites can be compared to emergency shelters for refugees, even though substandard temporary housing throughout the world is mainly used in response to natural or manmade disasters. Construction site shelters do not exist because of external forces like natural disasters or war, but rather due to manmade economic reasons and might be an example of space set up especially for temporary residents. In the construction industry prefabricated housing on site can be found wherever turbo urbanism has led to a construction boom and where the need to meet financial targets places an emphasis on quantity over quality. Living conditions such as those endured by workers in Chinese cities were typical for Europe during the Industrial Revolution, and are common in the United Arab Emirates today (Pattisson 2013). During the construction of Brasilia in 1960, the whole city layout was planned with the intention of meeting human needs, but the accommodation for the construction workers were completely forgotten (Scott 1998).

The consequences of rapid urbanism for those producing the buildings do not seem to be on the agenda when global urban hotspots and booming new cities are celebrated. Today, substandard housing conditions continue to be a reality in world cities. Charles Abrams astutely stated in 1946 that "Housing in the twentieth century has been one continuing emergency" (in Sinclair 2007: 39). UN-Habitat estimates that nearly one third of the world's urban population, around one billion people, live in housing conditions below human rights standard. This number is expected to double by 2030 (UN Habitat 2003 in Sinclair 2007). In many developing countries, rapid urbanization and industrialization has led to huge slums and shanty towns, but in China not many of these areas exist. When looking at Chinese construction site shelters in an international context, it is apparent that affordable on-site housing prevents China from having large-scale slum settlements (Wang Ya Ping/Wan Yanglin 2009). Precarious circumstances for construction workers can be found worldwide and while at first glance in Chinese cities there do not seem to be whole districts with substandard housing such as slums, there are huge numbers of people affected by these low living standards.

6.4 Social Situation

Without the housing possibilities offered on site, construction workers would not be able to afford to live in the city. Housing in the city is prohibitively expensive for the low-paid rural migrant workers as rising housing and other living costs make it increasingly difficult for migrant workers to cover basic expenses. Very little of their wages is left after deduction of food, other costs, and remittances that they send home. Most migrant workers are the main source of income for their entire family, but only see them 1-3 times a year for Chinese New Year and sometimes also for sowing and harvest, revealed on of the interviews in Kunshan.

As a result of internal migration, about 61 million children have currently been left behind in the countryside, of which about half live with one parent (CLB 2014). Migrant workers face the choice of either leaving their children behind in rural areas, where education is financed by the state due to their *hukou* registration, or educating them at city schools that they must pay for. Children who are left behind often face problems with learning and emotional development, but migrant schools in the city are often characterized by poor conditions, and teachers there usually work voluntarily. "The lack of affordable access to quality education for the children of rural migrants leaves them socially excluded, denies them the right to full development and violates their rights. Such inequality of opportunity can also lead to the intergenerational transmission of poverty and trigger further socioeconomic problems" (HDR China 2008: 97).

Because public services are tied to the place of *hukou* registration, families often end up living apart for many years. These lengthy separations are typically very stressful emotionally for both the person moving and for those left behind. Usually, mobility decisions are made by one household, not by the individual

(Fan 2008). As many migrant workers cannot afford to bring their families with them to the city in the male-dominated construction industry, women, children, and the elderly often stay behind in the rural village. On several construction site visits we witnessed evidence of disrupted family life when workers told us with sorrow how seldom they were able to travel home to their families. Sometimes women have to take care of children, grandparents, and farm work – or, in many cases the wife works in a factory and the grandparents look after the children and farm. However, during our research we repeatedly saw women living on construction sites. They were usually responsible for preparing food and doing the laundry for their workgroup, but they also carried out harsh work on the building site.

The Social Situation of Migrants in the City

"Accessing the urban is conceived not just as moving physically to cities, but also as appropriating and often reworking goods, ideas and trends associated with urbanity and urban life." (Ballew in Chen/Clark 2006: 225)

Economic reforms have reshaped traditional Chinese cities by transforming them into places of commerce and consumption and at the same time have created new patterns of social behaviour in their citizens. As Sassen (2001) has pointed out, the challenge facing China is to shift from a place of production to a producer service centre, to become a competitive player in the field of global capital. Skills and expertise are required for this to happen; as a result, China now foster nation-wide education and training programs.

Urban life has changed dramatically, which has resulted in new identities in Chinese city culture. In general, the perceptions of rural migrant workers, who came to the city in search of work, are somehow very negative. These perceptions have provoked a nationwide debate about *suzhi*, a term describing "the general level of the physique, intelligence, ideology, and ethics of the people of a country in the course of transforming nature and society" (Yan Hairong 2008: 113). Excluded from *hukou* benefits and social benefits, rural migrant workers are now also being accused of having a low *suzhi*. In this context rural usually stands for tradition and backwardness as opposed to urban, which is associated with modernity and cosmopolitism.

"[…] it has not only fortified institutional and social barriers between rural and urban China but also influenced all aspects of Chinese society and economy." (Fan 2008: 40)

No doubt, the *hukou* system is a primary reason for the disadvantaged position of rural migrants and the reason why low-skilled migrants are subject to economic and social segregation (Friedmann 2005). When analysing the impact of the *hukou* system as it relates to construction sites as places of residence, it becomes clear that one can plan the building process but not the fate of the participants. While the construction manager organizes prefabricated dorms for migrant construction workers during the building process, there are no plans made for the future. On which building site will the workers live after the current project is finished? And what will happen if city development slows down and rapid urbanization comes to an end? What will the consequences be for the workers?

Social implications and discrimination caused by the hukou system thus add to the already difficult circumstances of migrant construction workers. Currently there seem to be no strategies in place to deal with citizens who are not officially registered, who do not pay tax, but who need governmental support. This is likely exacerbating the problem and adding to the Chinese government's fear of an uprising by workers. As Cindy Fan (2008) suggests, the state prefers migrant workers to return to their rural homes without 'burdening the state', which references the urgent problem of dealing with the huge floating population. As rural-to-urban labour flows are still growing the household registration has been eased in recent years. A number of local governments have launched experimental programs to abolish or drastically limit the impact of the hukou system. However, the urban-rural gaps in public service delivery result from such deep-rooted systemic factors, that a number of other systematic reforms – like the Chinese Land Use Rights, are immediately affected (Shi Li 2010). However, since the 1990s there have been debates on how to reform the system or even to suggestions to put an end to the classification of rural and non-rural populations. A large international media debate in 2005 inaccurately predicted the end of the *hukou* registration system in China and "heralded the arrival of a new age of equal rural and urban rights and free migration, a dream for hundreds of millions of Chinese peasants over the past half century" (Chang Kam Wing/Buckingham 2008: 585).

An approach of abolishment of *hukou* divisions mainly occurred in small towns for local residents who were active in agriculture, but not nationwide. Since 2014 in some particular areas, urban and rural boundaries no longer exist, so people can move freely between city and country. This new unified *hukou* thus merged agricultural and non-agricultural *hukou* in each reformed area into one single category called *jumin hukou* (居民户口) and, for the first time, *hukou* documents seemed to give *mingong* the opportunity to work towards a better working and living environment, although this reform only occurred within the selected city or district and not nationwide (ibid.). These initiatives have led to several protests by peasants who resisted the land expropriation and were not satisfied with the compensation offered by local governments. Many peasants still prefer to keep their agricultural *hukou*, which include the right to own property and permission to have more than one child. The *hukou* reform initiative obviously does not meet the needs of the agricultural population at large, nor does it increase the standards of public welfare for them.

The registration system in China still has a major role in sustaining the supply of cheap labour, which impacts the global economy. The reforms have had a very marginal impact in terms of weakening the system, and the divisions between agricultural and non-agricultural populations remain just as the divide between locals and outsiders still exists (ibid.; Gaubatz 2010).

"Migrant worker is the synonym of low-quality in the society. I admit that we are the people living in the lowest level of the society. Even if we were paid attention to, we were seen as the weakest group. But now I do not feel worthless anymore, in fact we the migrant workers are also human beings, we are proud, all of the high-rise buildings are built up with our blood and sweat; we also are educated, I can write posts; we also know how to live. The reason I write this post is so everyone can know how we build a block of high-rise buildings, and also to show you our lives as migrant workers." (A young migrant construction worker, China Hush 2009)

Over the past 30 years rural migrants have made major contributions to the economic development of Chinese cities (Shi Li 2010). However, while many modern buildings have been recognized as architecturally notable, little attention is paid to the people who built them under such difficult conditions. Recently, the second generation of migrant workers has started adapting to their urban surroundings. They want to consume goods, feel entitled to services, and while their parents' generation saved all their hard earned money for remittances, the new generation is tempted to spend it. Migrant workers are starting to claim their rights, as several protests last year have shown (Pun Ngai/Xu Yi 2011). A serious engagement with the imperative of modernization should include structural changes in policies and, of course, a thorough analysis of the circumstances of rural workers.

Existing Strategies

Rural migration in China is a topic investigated by a vast body of literature that describes the disadvantaged circumstances of *mingong*, but findings on actual support strategies are less common. Many labour organizations founded to help improve the lives of working migrants are based in Hong Kong and are thus far away from many of the workers they are trying to help. According to Wemheuer (2011) there is no umbrella organization for NGOs in China. Their status is semi-legal; NGOs are neither prohibited nor officially approved. Many of these organizations are highly dependent on overseas funding since the Chinese government is generally suspicious of any specific groups formed to demand more rights. The few existing self-help organizations, as they are called in Chinese, provide legal consultation, rights advocacy, cultural education and entertainment, education in occupational health and safety, assistance in job seeking, help integrating migrant workers into urban life, and assistance with non-payment of wages and work injuries (Zhou Shaoqing 2011).

The main body of labour organizations in China are the trade unions. However, the leading organ of trade unions, the All-China Federation of Trade Unions (ACFTU), is part of the State machinery and as an organization that is affiliated to the government it places great emphasis on maintaining social stability. Thus, most migrant workers are left without effective support organizations to rely upon (ibid.). The NGOs and labour organizations that exist have difficulties reaching their target members as they have an uncertain legal status and are not recognized politically (Wemheuer 2011). According to Ding Li, vice director of the Non Profit Incubator (NPI) Shanghai, many private organizations do not register their existence, as there are strict regulations for NGOs (Krüger 2010). Most existing NGOs act without a legal registration and are tolerated as long as they do not challenge the Chinese authorities (Shieh 2015).

Within this mix of types of support organizations, several NGOs deserve to be mentioned in greater detail. The former migrant worker Wei Wei (2011) founded the organization *Xiao Xiao Niao* (小小鸟) for migrant workers as one of the few grassroots organizations defending their interests in 1999. He set up a hotline to help migrant workers seek justice, demanding compensation for injury or death, find employment, protect their rights, and demand unpaid salaries. In 2004 the Beijing Dongcheng District Bureau of Justice accepted Little Bird as a People's Mediation Committee, which enables members of the voluntary organization to offer on-the-spot counselling and mediation directly at construction sites. Likewise, Pun Ngai and Lu Huilin have started an initiative in cooperation with their students, who began to visit construction sites in *Lengquan Cun* (冷泉

村) close to Beijing on a regular basis to provide legal support in the local canteen. *Anquan Mao* (安全帽, protective helmet) as their initiative is called, also organizes afternoon care for children, movie nights, and other leisure activities for migrant workers. During an interview (Pun Ngai 2011) we were told that many of the workers have children in college, and therefore welcome the students helping them. "Respect for labour and labourers is a basic value of our country" are the words displayed in the entrance hall of the self-organized Culture and Arts Museum of Migrant Labourers, which has the mission of keeping a record of migrant workers' culture and history (Creischer/Hinderer/Siekmann 2010). The founder, Sun Heng, is a former migrant worker whose goal is "to advocate and promote migrant workers culture, to promote the recognition of the labour value, to foster and strengthen migrant workers' self-confidence and identity, so as to improve the overall living and working conditions of the migrant workers in China" (ibid.: 23). The intensification and extension of the urbanization process with all its societal side effects has led to various survival strategies and support programs, but the turning point where public opinion – including that of temporary residents – actually changes the way in which the urban environment is currently managed has yet to come.

Summary – Rural Urban Nomads

Working Conditions
The situation faced by rural migrant workers arriving in Shanghai stands in stark contrast to that of international migrants, as no comparable welcoming services are provided for the rural migrants. Becoming oriented and settled in the vast city happens mainly with the help of relatives already in town, or through fellow workers from the same place of origin. The job search and employment contracts work in the same way, which results in complex dependencies among family members and people from the same village that are based on trust. Generally, migrant workers endure extremely lengthy working hours that do not allow for sufficient rest overnight. The lack of mechanisms to ensure that labour rights are upheld leads to job exploitation on several levels: often workers are not paid the agreed-upon wages, have to work unpaid hours of overtime at night, and are subject to considerable uncertainty with regard to future work. They often have little savings left after sending remittances home to their families.

Living Conditions
The living conditions of migrant construction workers, like their working conditions, do not meet housing standards as defined by Article 25 of the Universal

Human Rights. The prefabricated dormitories on site, where construction workers tend to live, usually have no insulation and are far from meeting standards of decent living. They have one water source, which is usually outside, and no access to hot water. The shelters offer no privacy with up to six people living in one small room; additionally, living on site exposes them to enforcement by the employer. Just as construction sites are scattered throughout the city, substandard dwellings for workers are decentralized and not always immediately visible. An analysis of the degree of intermingling in urban spaces of rural construction workers is rather redundant, as the reasons for their isolated life within the city and for their non-use of public (open) space in Shanghai have been shown in detail in the previous chapters.

Social Situation

Given the situation of a rapidly growing construction sector enabled by over 40 million construction workers in China, it is incomprehensible that they still don't get social recognition for being the motor of the economic miracle since about 80% of urban growth in China is caused by rural-urban migration (Fan 2008). Due to *hukou* regulations, migrant workers are excluded from the social benefits provided by the state, and regional differences in social insurance prevent highly mobile migrant workers from effectively insuring themselves. In conclusion, it is obvious that minimum standards of human rights and labour regulations are consistently violated by the existing working conditions on construction sites in and around Shanghai. The integration of these migrants into urban life seems long overdue if the objective is ensuring the existence of a humane urban environment. The intensification and extension of the urbanization process with all its side effects for the people involved has led to various survival strategies and support programs, but the turning point where public opinion – including temporary residents – is actually changing the ways in which the urban environment is currently managed, has yet to come.

7. Reflecting on Urban Nomads

This chapter is an interpretation and reflection of the findings of our study. We seek to situate our results in a wider context, starting with a breakdown of the small-scale phenomena discussed and then broadening the focus to include a larger-scale view. One aim is to contextualize this analysis within existing research in order to uncover potential gaps and to provide an overview of future research questions. Reflecting the two case studies and the limitations of our empirical approach, we are well aware that we have provided deep insight into a small number of the many aspects of the urban phenomena occurring in China's cities. Social reality can be approached from many different angles, thus we had to make the difficult decision of which scientific approach to take to best illuminate the urban phenomenon of migrants within the construction process in Shanghai. As described in the research methods of both case studies, we chose different approaches for the two social groups, including participant observation, ethnographic research, and action research. Following Bryman, ethnography and participant observation are difficult to distinguish from one another: "Both draw attention to the fact that the participant observer/ethnographer immerses him- or herself in a group for an extended period of time observing behaviour, listening to what is said in conversations both between others and with the fieldworker, and asking questions" (Bryman 2004: 292).

During our fieldwork we realized that being just participant observers was not possible; by interacting with the observed people – both rural and global migrants – we were able to obtain many additional useful details. We played a range of different roles during the research process varying from outsider to insider, depending on who we were talking to. These interactions also clearly influenced the results, since the reactions of the people we were speaking to were influenced by their perceptions of us and our roles. The observed target groups often showed interest in us as well as in our approach to issues relating to architecture, construction, project management, and migration.

The aim of the two case studies was not to use a holistic approach, as there is no single theory that describes all urban phenomena; rather, multiple theories need to be used to approach the complex urban field in its entirety. By questioning the latest developments in contemporary urban China we addressed relevant problems in planning practice, but again the great complexity of Chinese urbanism cannot be addressed with a single, all-encompassing solution. Nevertheless, the aim was to give a broad spectrum of perspectives on the urbanization process in Shanghai through the two case studies. By showing examples of everyday life we linked our micro-level observations to different scales at the meso and macro level. The two case studies thus do not describe one specific moment in the Chinese urban realm, but rather seek to illuminate life in the transforming city, challenges for mobile inhabitants, and people in transition. To be a working migrant means something different in every country and culture. Work is usually linked to the national legal framework and to general working conditions, which are regulated and controlled by the state, companies, and society. Within this book and in the case of the observed groups – internal and global working migrants in China – it is especially important to understand the local market situation, and in particular the political and the economic control mechanisms of the urban environment. Due to the fact that migrants live in a new environment without the support of their family, friends, and familiar environment, they find themselves in a very difficult position in which to formulate their individual needs.

7.1 Reflecting on Global Urban Nomads

Migration is the key driver of urban change worldwide. It is also responsible for new patterns of urban diversity, and will pose particular social and political challenges in China due to the country's status as a global growing market. After analyzing the current situation of global nomads on the social, spatial and working level in China, we have come to the conclusion that even though expatriates have social and economic capital that gives them privileged status in society, they still remain foreign in certain ways. As a result, they inhabit "social bubble worlds", which lead to further spatial segregation in Shanghai. However, we believe that there is great potential for positive change on all three levels that we have addressed in our core propositions.

Keeping our findings in mind, we are convinced – even if they are only temporary residents – possess the ideas and tools to demand solutions to existing problems and to begin implementing them in the city. They can thus act as visionaries and collaborative participants in the cities in which they live, which can enable them to find their place in the receiving society. We have demonstrated that approaches are being developed that react spatially to the needs of an increasingly mobile society. Here a shift in perception on the part of the receiving society – the Chinese – as well on the part of the immigrating society – the expatriates – is needed. As urban participants, and as global urban nomads, they should be perceived as individuals with equal rights instead of being treated as outsiders in city life. We thus call for a shift in perception that sees global expatriates as active users of the city and participants who claim new forms of temporal dwelling according to their explicit and implicit spatial needs. This is a call for the temporary right to space for global nomads.

In this sense, we firmly believe that expatriates are permanent temporary urban residents who should be integrated into local life and not just into global business. Even though permanent settlements are an essential characteristic of cities, architects should search for solutions that include the needs of today's flexible life amid the jungle of buildings. This could result in a dwelling for the contemporary expatriate that would allow him or her to easily participate in the new urban environment. Therefore, we are arguing for a shift in the production of housing and public spaces: they should be perceived as global communities, as places of multicultural interaction within a common framework. They could transform into places for the exchange of cultures, and could act as a catalyst for integration in the constantly changing Chinese urban landscape.

Based on these observations, planners should take the potential benefits of mixing and cultural exchange into consideration. In functionalism and pragmatic approaches the field of architecture globalization and connectivity are key words, yet architects' and urban planners' main role is to divide space into zones dedicated to particular functions. Cowan argues that architects can provide more "leadership to societies in the development of livable environments, whether fixed, permanent and solitary, or portable, temporary, and communal" (Cowan 2002: 3). Therefore, one major role of the architects is to engage in a dialogue and share concepts and experiences with regard to environmental issues.

7.2 REFLECTING ON RURAL URBAN NOMADS

During our observations of rural migrant workers, we first highlighted the individuals and their way of life, then investigated their immediate surroundings and living conditions, and finally viewed their circumstances with close attention to the social, political, and legal issues that greatly influence the lives of rural construction workers in the city. By taking a closer look at the current situation we have gained new insight and encountered several issues that will remain unresolved in this book. The problems we have pointed out exist on several levels – sociospatial, structural, educational, and cultural – and most of these difficulties are caused in large part by the permanent temporariness of migrant workers. Without local *hukou* registration, a better living and working situation seems difficult to achieve under the current system. This separation between *hukou* registration place and the actual living place seems to be the cause of many disadvantages. Some possible and necessary changes would also have a major impact on other areas, for example changing *hukou* regulations implies changing the Land Use Rights accordingly. At the moment, even if many of these issues are a result of political decisions, there are surprisingly few alternative strategies to strengthen the position of migrant construction workers in the city.

Everyone should have the right to security and is entitled to the realization of their economic, social, and cultural rights (Universal Declaration of Human Rights Article 22). Even though China's cities have few slums, prefabricated containers do not meet standards of decent housing. When considering the vast quantity of construction site shelters that are spread throughout Shanghai, it becomes clear that precarious living conditions, such as in slums, are decentralized rather than absent. Under the existing circumstances we see potential for improvement on all three levels that we have addressed in our core propositions. Rural urban nomads should be perceived as individuals with equal rights instead of as a cheap labour force building our cities. Therefore we call for new forms of temporary dwelling according to the explicit and implicit spatial needs of migrant construction workers, thus for their temporary right to space and the ability to participate in the city life.

In the context of this book the term low-skilled describes workers who are less educated or earn low wages due to their lack of access to education. Our call for better circumstances for migrant workers should not be understood as accusing workers of having no skills. We are also not calling for an increase in the productivity of these workers. It might be helpful to provide training programs that empower rural workers to strengthen their working skills and expertise through a network of professional trainers – to give them the opportunity to improve their social status within Chinese urban society. Here, we are again referring to the capability approach, which envisions a more equally developed society where knowledge and capital are distributed in a way that is different from the vast inequalities that currently characterize Shanghai.

7.3 INTERRELATIONS BETWEEN URBAN NOMADS

Our analysis was situated at three different levels within dynamic urban space. We refined these levels with three hypotheses. By looking back at these core propositions we offer a broader perspective on our research results and place them within the context of architectural practice.

Hypothesis 1: Tailor-Made City Planning

Large Scale – Urban Layer – the Excluded User
The transformation of urban space is not only visible in the flood of new construction, but can also be seen in the transformation of urban culture. This includes seeing Chinese urbanism as a new way of life. While society adapts quickly to new circumstances (for example, working migrants and specialists from abroad recognize and take advantage of opportunities), architecture does not seem to take the resulting new requirements of temporary life into account during the process of architectural production. When conducting research on temporary residents of Shanghai, no matter which circumstances led them to being temporary, it becomes obvious that the social status of being guests or outsiders in the city allows them no political voice in decisions.

Expatriates have been discovered as consumers of support services, media, and residential compounds and other enclosed spaces, but their needs as temporary citizens within the urban realm are not sufficiently taken into account by designers and decision-makers. Depending on the planning systems in question – public or private – foreigners only influence projects where affluent consumers are the target group. Purpose-built and tailor-made areas are only for selected consumer groups. Even though permanent settlements are an essential characteristic of cities, architects and planners should search for solutions including the needs of today's flexible life in the jungle of solid buildings. In this sense we claim to accept that expatriates are permanent temporary urban residents, who should be integrated into the local life and not just into the global business. Beyond this, we believe that expats are more than a consumer group reliant upon capital; they are permanently temporary urban citizens, and this status calls for their further sustained social, political, economic, and spatial engagement.

Although migrant workers are building the city, they have not managed to create a visible and empowered urban nomadic society; the migrants are usually invisible and marginalized in architectural culture and discourse as well as in practice. They are disadvantaged when compared to local urban citizens and are not sufficiently considered part of the public by politicians, architects, and planners. As city planning in Shanghai does not succeed in meeting the requirements of the latest developments in migration flows, it is clear that migrant working is not considered in municipal city planning. The basic human rights of decent living and working conditions are not regulated for them by the formal system and, while global urban nomads are often able to compensate for the lack of state benefits at their own cost, rural urban nomads cannot afford this kind of support on their own.

In this book we argue that city planning should consider the needs of both investigated groups to foster their contributions to city life. The human potential of cities is determined by users of the city; these users are intimately implicated in the potential of these cities to provide the benefits of better urban and social infrastructure to their residents.

Hypothesis 2: Cocooned Living

Medium Scale – Living Environment – The Excluded Consumer
The two groups we observed are spatially clustered in bubble worlds within the city, although the way this is manifested is quite different. Foreign residences have become synonymous with high-quality living, and not only foreigners but also wealthier Shanghainese and new Shanghainese with a desire for status have shown that they prefer to live in gated communities, as they offer safety and a community of shared lifestyles.

In Shanghai, foreign communities historically clustered in gated communities. These residential high-rise complexes and low-rise villa compounds with private gardens were developed out of necessity, but later these foreign settlements led to a new housing market. The socio-spatial exclusion revealed in these residential developments continues into everyday life and leads to a parallel foreign world within Shanghai. For many housing researchers, gated communities conflict with personal politics and wider ideals in terms of trying to achieve a social balance in neighbourhoods and ensuring social justice.

Referring to our observations on global urban nomads, architecture should take potentials of mixture and cultural exchange into consideration: a dwelling for a contemporary expatriate to participate in the new urban environment in future. Therefore a shift in perception of the gated communities to global communities should be considered, places of multicultural interaction within a common framework – a transformation into places for exchange of cultures, which act as a catalyst for integration in the constantly changing Chinese urban landscape.

Similarly, we argue that rural migrants tend to live in cocoon worlds within the city. Rising housing prices and living costs make it increasingly difficult for rural migrant workers to cover basic expenses, and thus the only affordable housing for workers is often provided by the employer. We object to these on-site housing structures as they do not meet standards of decent housing, nor do they consider rural urban nomads' needs. Providing affordable housing for low income workers coming to the city is a challenge. Enclosed aspects of urban residences for temporary dwellers are defined by gates, walls, guards, and significant distances from the city centre, factors which lead to difficulties with urban integration and, further, to exclusion from public space in Shanghai. When listening to the needs of rural migrant workers, not the prefabricated houses would be symptomatic of China's ongoing modernization process, but a spatial organization and design that is maybe more similar to international programs for affordable housing including social housing subsidies.

Hypothesis 3: Working challenges

Small Scale – Building Projects – Issues Among the Involved
Conversations about recent construction projects in China often involve discussions of the low quality of the buildings. In particular, foreigners involved in the buildings' planning and design often complain about the poor execution of their projects. Beyond the debate on the quality of the buildings that are erected at such enormous speed, it is often forgotten that the construction process is more than just the materialized end result. Further observation of individual construction phases shows that many construction workers are faced with challenging tasks for which they have not been prepared. Lacking specialized training and often also without much education, rural migrants have difficulty performing these jobs to a high standard. About 80 percent of construction workers in Chinese cities lack these advanced skills and relevant education, which leads to further disadvantages in terms of promoting self-sufficiency to improve the social status of these workers. Based on the conviction that building quality will improve in the long term if adequate education is provided for rural migrant workers, and better cultural understanding of global migrant workers is encouraged, we propose at this point, to already begin the prevention of the construction of

buildings that still leave much to be desired. As there are so many different stakeholders associated with the construction process, it is now more important than ever that all parties have the skills necessary to understand and effectively communicate with each other in light of the different resources and circumstances involved.

7.4 Urban Nomads' Right to Shanghai

In terms of the position of our book among other scientific work, the multi layered approach we have taken has engaged with several areas of research within the interdisciplinary field of critical urban studies. Our research bridges the disciplines of urban studies, project management, business studies, and migration research. By doing so our intent was to forge a link between existing investigations and the present work.

When drawing on urban studies one of the core arguments is that space is not just a (material) object, nor is it a pure idea; it is also a societal process of production (Lefebvre 2009 [1974]). Thus the main focus lies in the relationships between the production of the built environment and the people who are involved in the construction process. In the context of the study we highlight the influence of permanently temporary urban participants in Shanghai on the production of space as a social phenomenon. Much work in migration studies has described in detail the divergent circumstances of migrant workers worldwide and within China. In an approach that differs from typical research on migrants, we have emphasised two aspects of these workers' mobility: a survival-based decision of people with no alternative combined with a strategic choice made by individuals actively realizing their identities. Also in this context, we have focused on the exceptional nature of the observed social groups, who are both not only migrants but also permanently temporary residents.

The rapid transformation of the urban environment is often described from an angle of economics and business studies with focus on quantitative facts. Although very precise in providing statistical data, these surveys do not consider the social and cultural aspects of this urban development. By referring to the discipline of project management, which sees construction as a process, we point out the necessity to also consider the needs of the actors involved in the process. We have taken an approach that combines scholarship from the above-mentioned disciplines, which has helped us to grasp the complex urban development occurring in Shanghai and has enabled us to make this book a critical urban study. Furthermore, we had special access to the research field by approaching it from two sides at the same time. Various perspectives on two such different – but also similar – groups of working migrants gave us the opportunity to look at them from different angles.

During our research in Shanghai, we were confronted with various situations for which we were not prepared. There were various difficulties encountered in the course of our research, questions that could not yet be answered, and other issues we experienced. Our focus on two very different groups demonstrates the exceptional nature of our research, but at the same time the huge economic, cultural, and social gaps between the two observed groups has been quite a challenge. Educated as architects, constantly switching between such extreme situations was difficult when observing such delicate urban and human phenomena.

As the research field turned out to be unfathomably large and extremely complex, it would be appropriate to conduct further research now, which would allow us to expand upon the findings and the knowledge gained since we began the process. Further research fields are endless in this sector and many more topics in the Chinese urban realm could be the subject of follow up projects. Some topics have appeared during our research that seem especially relevant for further studies. As architects we learn to deal with the desires of users and of the live objectives of city residents but our education doesn't yet consider the social aspect within the construction process.

In this context research in the future should include possibilities of how to avoid low-quality dwellings on site and how to develop further strategies for affordable housing in Chinese cities. Migrant construction workers of course find themselves positioned between their own precarious living conditions and the buildings they are erecting. Dealing with the topics of labour migration, multi-culturalism, and the diversity of local and transnational identities remains a challenging issue in Shanghai over the next few years. Hence it remains necessary to further encourage intercultural exchange in planning as well as long-term project implementation. Increasing awareness of cultural and social issues among architects, urban planners, and designers could lead to cities being shaped not only by economic and political decisions but by a greater focus on the inhabitants' needs. We strongly advocate and support such an approach and call for an urbanism that responds to the needs of 'permanently temporary urban participants'.

To us, architecture is more than form, material and design. We understand architecture as a social, economic and political process and see the architect more in the role of a generalist than a specialist, and, in the particular case of China, as a cultural mediator too. To open a cultural dialogue it is important not to oppose either the eastern or the western positions, but to establish and investigate parallels so that conclusions for progress can be drawn.

8. Prospects

> "Social sustainability for a city is defined as development (and/or growth) that is compatible with the harmonious evolution of civil society, fostering an environment conductive to the compatible cohabitation of culturally and socially diverse groups, while at the same time encouraging social integration, with improvements in the quality of life for all segments of population."
>
> (STREN/POLÈSE IN MILGROM/KROLL 2008: 268)

8.1 FAIR BUILDING

Presented as snapshots of the contemporary transformation of urban China, with migration understood as driving force that defines new goals and tasks, this book can be seen as an attempt to provide insights into the complex process of the production of built space in contemporary China. After we have shown various examples of the conditions under which buildings are erected in China, we will add the question of whether there are strategies to improve the current situation to some extent and, if so, what that would involve. In the book we have given an overview of contemporary political, economic, and social debates related to labour issues in China; we have considered these in the context of architectural and construction practice. As pointed out in the previous chapters, inadequate safety standards, unreasonable working conditions, and unequal distribution of income, power, and knowledge among the involved are common practice within the hierarchical structure of the construction business. Thus, it is our objective to raise awareness, to demand improvements to the present situation of Chinese migrant construction workers and encourage action. These improvements include the need for increasing wages, implementation of safety regulations, trade union participation, social insurance benefits, and better working and living conditions overall. Therefore the following questions urgently need to be addressed beyond this work: How can better working and living conditions be ensured, adopted, and realized by all parties concerned? What are possible control mechanisms? And, of particular importance, who is responsible for ensuring compliance with these regulations such as a code of professional ethics? Moreover, the examples of Chinese construction processes demonstrate a lack of international understanding of socially just building practice.

In the context of this work we aim to outline some possible ways to improve the depicted working and living conditions based on different participants and their potential actions. We are convinced that the concept *Fair Building* is able to add a social layer to the ongoing debate on sustainable building performance. This includes the idea to promote the transfer of concepts like Fair Trade to the construction industry. While a trend toward sustainable urban development has become measurable through certifications like LEED, BREEAM and China Green Building Label, the idea *Fair Building* promotes the need for the ability to track building processes and building transactions on a social level. The observations of this study have revealed that the organizational structure on construction sites is hierarchical and highly dependent on cheap labour. However, construction is not only about the end result; it is also about the process, conditions, and circumstances under which space is created and, further, how it is used. Here an approach on multiple levels shows some possibilities of how to intervene in the current practice. Increasing awareness must take place among all different stakeholders involved in the process, starting with the client, planners, managers, executing companies, private enterprises, trainers, and future residents of the building.

The key features of our proposed *Fair Building* approach address the issues on three different levels:

- Production level (for construction workers): sustainable building, including decent conditions and vocational education for workers, controlled by members of the *Fair Building* network
- Intersection level (for architects): architects who are willing to participate in a fair process and actively support the agreed-upon guidelines
- Consumption level (for end-users): end users and clients who are proud to use and/or finance a building that is produced in a fair manner

Figure 24: Fair Building – Three Level Approach:

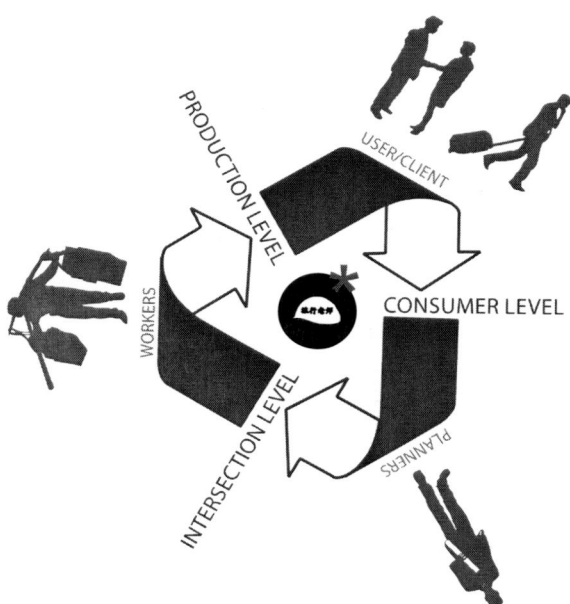

Source. Illustration Bronner | Reikersdorfer 2011

This illustration may provide the basic idea of how to have an impact on three levels simultaneously. In the following sections we will detail what that means for the different actors involved in the construction process.

The Production Level

Residential design began to address the physical health of urban inhabitants with the Modern movement. Driven by the environmental awareness that followed in the 1960s and 1970s, "designers developed more detailed understandings of ecological processes and the impacts that urban forms have on the environment" (Milgrom/Kroll 2008: 267). Standards that measure urban sustainability have been defined for these environmental components of cities, and to prove that production is sustainable, particular certificates have been introduced. This demonstrates the current trend wherein architects and end clients focus on the quality of the product. Raising awareness about environmental issues and sustainability has also found application in China. This is demonstrated through the development of a national label called China Green Building Label (Three Star) based on the international certificate Leadership in Energy and Environmental

Design (LEED) for sustainable and green building practice. Furthermore, the Chinese government has encouraged the transfer of know-how and technology in the field of sustainable building practice through international cooperative arrangements. While we support the on-going green building process, we believe that in addition to ecological discussion there is a need to investigate further in social standards of the production of the built environment. As social and environmental aspects are highly interconnected, we suggest considering socially conscious building criteria together with green building certifications.

The Planning Party

The previous observation of construction processes has shown on the one hand that many construction workers face challenging tasks they have not been prepared for and on the other hand that engagement on the part of planners is lacking, which further reinforces this conflict. No matter where one is working and which labour regulations exist in that country, planners and architects need to assume social responsibility. Here we refer to the Architects Code Standards of Professional Conduct and Practice, a code of professional ethics for architects and planners by the Architecture Registration Board in the UK: "You are expected to observe this Code wherever in the world you work" (ARB 2010). By promoting compliance with Western working standards, architects should be prepared to support an improvement of working standards for the participants involved when working globally. In this context, it is clear that it is also the responsibility of the planning party (project developers, architects, designers, structural engineers, etc.) to stand up for fairer working conditions and better training for construction workers.

The sense of urgency that something needs to be done may lead architects to become more socially engaged in construction processes. Social responsibility within the complex construction process – involving participants with widely varying characteristics – needs to be approached at multiple levels. We propose interventions at a professional and educational level. Professionally, the impact should be made at the level of the professional organization that regulates the architectural profession. With the ongoing trend of architects to work all over the world, university education should prepare students for working globally by intercultural training and promoting compliance with western working standards abroad. Hence this is a claim for architectural education to take more practical aspects of global working challenges into consideration to raise awareness through cultural exchange programs for mutual understanding.

Consumer Awareness

In the third level of our approach to *Fair Building*, we address the clients and end users. Certifications of transparent processes help the consumer to make socially conscious decisions. Thus, customers and developers could have an incentive to use or finance a building that has been produced in a fair process that takes the whole value chain into account. The Fair Trade Foundation is a prime example to demonstrate "alternatives to conventional trade and other forms of advocacy, the Fairtrade movement empowers citizens to campaign for an international trade system based on justice and fairness" (Fair Trade Vision 2011). The intention of the Fair Trade Foundation is to transform trading structures and production chains by facilitating trading partnerships based on equity and transparency. The certification is exclusively given to companies that comply with international standards and contractual requirements to provide end consumers with the opportunity to actively make value-based choices by labelling their products as Fair Trade. By referring to the example of Fair Trade the idea is to enable clients and users to make a consumer choice based on a fair production process. The improvement of overall social standards is a long-term goal of the Fair Building initiative and further promotes better working conditions for people involved in the construction process. Nevertheless, this requires awareness and willingness to take action – on both the employers' side and the consumer's side – in order to get individuals to take more responsibility for the social implications of their actions.

8.2 FROM IDEA TO ACTION

> 授人以鱼 三餐之需 授人以渔 终生之用
> *"Give a fish to a man, he has food for a day.*
> *Teach a man to fish, he learns a skill for life."*
> CHINESE SAYING

This strategy shows possible ways to resolve social concerns by creating various opportunities and chances for those involved.

- Address relevant problems (intention formation)
- Find innovative solutions (idea development – start up initiative)
- Scale new ideas and create lasting ventures (running operation)
- Create positive social impact (impact scaling)

Throughout our research we have contemplated how we, who at the time were not directly involved in any construction processes, could go a step beyond simply describing the present circumstances. Following the approach of Social Entrepreneurship we found a way to position ourselves with our concept 移动课堂 – *Yidong Ketang*, which aims to improve the social consequences of the production of space. As pointed out in our third hypothesis, the lack of sufficient education and training often results in poor building quality. During one of the first visits to a construction site in 2010, we witnessed a discussion between a construction manager and a migrant construction worker about the necessity of overlapping waterproof sheeting in a fountain in the entrance area. Due to the lack of a common language – culturally as well as subject-specific – they failed to reach a consensus on the details. It is common knowledge that buildings are being erected at an enormous speed in Shanghai and that quality is often compromised in order to meet deadlines and reduce cost. Derogatory remarks about the standards of building, which often only represent a minimum level of quality, are quite frequent when working in China. Awareness is growing that current development trends are causing huge environmental problems, and the building industry in particular contributes to increasing energy consumption.

As we have detailed in the previous chapters we focus here on the people implement promising concepts, often at their own cost and without the necessary preparations. Our concept of a portable classroom presents an intervention that may be regarded as a possible way to implement *Fair Building*. When aiming to tackle the core of this problem, we need to delve a bit deeper. As a result of our detailed analysis of the current situation of rural migrant workers, and the position of global working migrants within the construction process, it is our intention to find innovative solutions to create a positive social impact, additional benefits, and a higher social value for the construction business. Relying on our observations, the already existing examples of good practice like the Fair Trade Foundation, Green Building Certification Labels, and the Code of Conduct are potential solutions, as is the recently unveiled concept of *Fair Building*. In response to this we have developed the concept *Yidong Ketang* – a mobile classroom. Our idea is to establish a training program for migrant construction workers in order to strengthen their working skills. We propose to do this by setting up a part-time education centre in a vocational school that focuses on building trades and handcrafting skills. This training empowers migrant workers to specialize in various fields of building and draws upon a network of teachers, international trainers, NGOs, and other experts. By involving decision-making parties such as clients, construction companies, and other building institutions the goal is to gain their attention, interest, and support.

As the focus of the training is on practical skills, the school will be situated on or close to the building site. Similar to the migrants themselves, who are highly mobile, the school is a portable teaching environment, and can move among construction sites in the city. The program can be set up in different iterations that consist of several phases and are based on an overall plan. This flexible module system can be adjusted to local needs at different construction sites. We envision that teaching will happen on a single evening or day at first. Instead of "learning by doing" the workers will receive a short introduction to the next working task in a single classroom on site. Based on the belief that the migrant working class should be supported by worker education and training, the concept of the vocational school is designed to respond to local needs. Complex quality-related problems seem to be closely related to the individual skills of the participants in the construction process. Offering specialist training courses in crafts and technical training will thus close a gap in the current educational system. Additionally, the program aims to enhance workers' chances, improve their social status, and thus also create better job opportunities. At the same time, a stronger personal willingness to improve the construction process will have a positive impact on building quality in the long term.

The training program aims to provide adequate education for rural migrant workers and encourages improved cultural understanding of global migrant workers. By providing the needed infrastructure in the city, by intensifying existing networks, and by providing the opportunity for regular and spontaneous interaction, the mobile classroom supports migrant workers involved in the construction process and helps them to determine the course of their own lives. Based on the conviction that working and living conditions, as well as building quality, will be improved in the long term by providing adequate education and safety regulations for rural migrant workers, and by encouraging stronger cultural understanding of global migrants involved in the construction process, we strongly emphasize that the training programme must be counteracted at an early stage of the building process. As there are so many different involved in the construction process, it is now more important than ever that those involved have the skills necessary to understand and communicate with one another in a transcultural dialogue.

Figure 25: Map of Shanghai

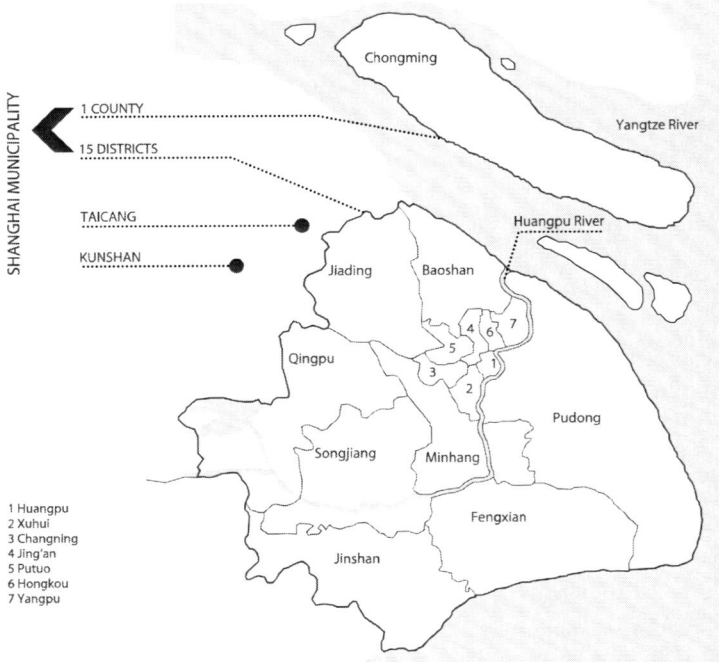

Source. Illustration Bronner | Reikersdorfer 2011

Acknowledgement

We would like to express our gratitude to everyone who supported us throughout the course of this research project, who talked things over with us, read, wrote, offered comments, assisted in the editing, proofreading and design. We extend our thanks to the involved firms for their close cooperation and we would like to thank our contributors, including the State of Vorarlberg (Land Vorarlberg). Furthermore, we are most appreciative to the various international and rural migrant workers who were available for interviews, shared their stories with us and provided glimpses into their lives. We further express our warm thanks to Sabine Knierbein for her professional advice and guidance. In the process of selecting and editing we were supported by Catherine Cowell, Marlene Reikersdorfer and Markus Rhomberg, to whom we would like to express our thanks and recognition. Above all we are sincerely thankful to our partners and families for their prolonged encouragement, patience and help during the whole process.

Glossary

Chinese terms as well as names of people and places are transliterated by the Hanyu Pinyin system in the text and highlighted in the form of italic type. A list of the Romanized terms and names and their corresponding Chinese characters is provided in the glossary.

This book follows the Chinese convention for names, putting the family name first, except in citations to certain works published in English

Monetary values are generally stated in Chinese currency Renminbi (RMB).

ānquán mào	安全帽	protection helmet (initiative to support migrant workers in Beijing)
bāo gōngtóu	包工头	lowest subcontractor, searching for working groups
biān zuò biān xué	边做边学	learning by doing
chéngzhōng cūn	城中村	urban villages
dàbāo	大包	contractor
dǎgōng	打工	work
dài gong	代工代工	group leader
dānwèi	单位	working unit
fēngshuǐ	风水	Chinese concept for harmony, literally "wind-water"

hǎiguī	海归	return migrant, also being called sea turtle
hǎiguī	海龟	sea turtle, also meaning returnee
hùkǒu	户口	household registration system
jūmín hùkǒu	居民户口	unified hukou
Kūnshān	昆山	a county level city in the greater Suzhou region
lǎobǎn	老板	boss
Lěngquán cūn	冷泉村	Cold Spring Village close to Beijing
liáng piào	粮票	food coupons
lǐlòng	里弄	literally "lanes and alleys" referring to neighborhood of lanes populated by houses which had evolved since its creation from 1842 to about 1949
méiyǒu bǐ línshí yímín gèng yǒngjiǔ de.	没有比临时移民更永久的。	"There is nothing as permanent as a temporary migrant."
nóngmíngong	农民工	peasant migrant workers
rén hù fēnlí	人户分离	family separation
rénmínbì	人民币	Chinese currency
rùjìng wèn sú	入境问俗	when you enter a country enquire about the local customs
Shànghǎi	上海	Shanghai
shítáng	食堂	canteen
Shòu rén yǐ yú sān cān zhī xū shòu rén yǐ yú zhōngshēng zhī yòng.	授人以鱼三餐之需 授人以渔 终生之用。	Give a fish to a man, he has food for a day. Teach a man to fish, he learns a skill for life.

sùshè	宿舍	dormitory
sùzhì	素质	innate quality; here referring to "human quality"
Tàicāng	太仓	a county level city in the greater Suzhou region
tiānxià wūyā yìbān hēi	天下乌鸦一般黑	all crows are black under the sky
wàidìrén	外地人	outsider
wàixiāo fang	外销房	foreign housing; export housing
wèishéme	为什么	why
wǒ shì yī zhī xiǎo xiǎo niǎo	我是一只小小鸟	"I am just a little bird"
xiàhǎi	下海	literally entering the sea referring to China's open door policy
xiǎo xiǎo niǎo dǎgōng hùzhù rèxiàn - hànwèi míngōng quányì	打工互助热线 - 捍卫民工权益	Little Bird workers' help hotline – defending migrant workers' rights
xiǎomàibù	小卖部	little kiosk
Yídòng kètáng	移动课堂	mobile classroom
yīnyáng	阴阳	Yin and Yang
yuan	元	yuan

Bibliography

A.T Kearney China (2010): City FDI Attractiveness IndexTM 2010. Trends Affecting Global Investment Strategies in China. http://www.atkearney.de/content/misc/wrapper.php/id/51119/name/pdf_trends_affecting_global_investment_strategies_in_china_12807601748344.pdf [accessed 04 May 2011]

ACS (2014): American Club of Shanghai. www.acshanghai.org [accessed 30 September 2014]

Agustin, Laura (2003): Forget Victimization: Granting agency to migrants. In development, Society for International Development, 46(3), 30-36.

AHK (2001): China, Delegations of German Industry & Commerce, http://china.ahk.de/de/ [accessed 25 September 2011]

Alpermann, Björn (2011): Bauer, Händler, Produktpirat Soziale Identitäten in China im Wandel. Regieren in China. Background Paper No. 5/2011.

Amnesty International Report (2010): The state of the world's human rights. 27 May 2010. http://report2010.amnesty.org/ [accessed 09 May 2011]

Ānquán mào (2011): NGO Safety Helmet. http://wiki.china.org.cn/wiki/index.php/Safety_Helmet [accessed 07 October 2011]

Aon Hewitt (2010): Expatriate, Returnee and China Hired Foreigner, Compensation and Benefits Survey. Result Sharing Presentation. The American Chamber of Commerce in Shanghai.

ARB (2010): Architecture Registration Broad, UK. Architects Code: Standards of Conduct and Practice. www.arb.org.uk/code-of-conduct-2010 [accessed 28 September 2011]

Atkinson, Rowland/Blandly, Sarah (2005): Introduction. International Perspectives on the New Enclavism and the Rise of Gated Communities, Housing Studies, Vol. 20, No. 2, 177-186.

Awe, Thomas (2007): Der verzweifelte Marsch in die Stadt. Shanghai und das Phänomen der Migration, Sankt Augustin: Konrad-Adenauer-Stiftung e.V.

Balfour, Alan/Shiling, Zheng (2002): World Cities: Shanghai (World Cities Series), London: Academy Press.

Bergère, Marie-Claire (2010): Shanghai: China's Gateway to Modernity; Stanford, Claif.: Stanford University Press.

Beynon, David (2008): Refusal of Home? Architecture Ex-Patriota, Interstices, vol. 9, pp. 9-21, Auckland, N.Z.: Enigma Publications.

Bradshaw, Michael/Stenning, Alison (2004): East Central Europe and the former Soviet Union: The Post-Socialist States (Drag Regional Development Series: no.5). Harlow: Prentic Hall.

Bray, David. (2009). Governing Urban China: Labour Welfare and the Danwei. In L. Tomba, A. Kipnis, J. Unger (Eds.), Contemporary Chinese Society and Politics, (pp. 105-136). London & New York: Routledge imprint of Taylor & Francis.

Brenner, Neil/Marcuse, Peter/Mayer, Margit (2009): Cities for people, not for profit. London: Routledge.

Brenner, Neil/Peck, Jamie/Nik, Theodore (2009): Neoliberal Urbanism. Models, Moments, Mutations. Baltimore, Maryland: The Johns Hopkins University Press SAIS Review - Volume 29, Number 1, pp. 49-66.

Bridge, Gary/Waston, Sophie (eds.) (2011): The New Blackwell Companion to the City. West Sussex, UK: Blackwell Publishing.

Bryman, Alan (2004): Social Research Methods, Second Edition. New York: Oxford University Press Inc.

Burdett, Ricky/Sudjic, Deyan (eds.) (2011): Living in the Endless City. The Urban Age Project by the London School of Economics and Deutsche Bank's Alfred Herrhausen Society. London: Phaidon Press Limited.

Campanella, Thomas J. (2008): The Concrete Dragon. China's Urban Revolution and What it Means for the World. New York: Princeton Architectural Press.

Chen, Nancy/Clark, Constance D. (eds.) (2006): China Urban. Ethnographies of Contemporary Culture. Durham&London: Duke University Press.

China Hush (2009): A construction migrant worker's notes. http://www.chinahush.com/2009/11/29/a-construction-migrant-workers-notes/ [accessed on 04 September 2011

China Perspectives (2010): Special Feature: Rural Migrants: On the Fringe of the City, a Bridge to the Countryside. Hong Kong: Hop Sze Printing, 2010/4.

China Review (2011): http://cnreviews.com [accessed 30 September 2011]

CHIPS (2002): China Household Income Project Survey. In China Perspectives 2010/4, Hong Kong: Hop Sze Printing, 2010.

CLB – China Labour Bulletin (2011): Wages in China 2011. http://www.china-labour.org.hk/en, [accessed 09 July 2011]

CLB – China Labour Bulletin (2016): Migrant Workers and their Children. http://www.clb.org.hk/en/view-resource-centre-content/110306 [accessed on 28 January 2016]

COMPAS (2011): Centre on Migration, Policy and Society, http://www.compas.ox.ac.uk/ [accessed 28 September 2011]

Cowan, Gregory (2002): Nomadology in Architecture. Empherality, Movement and Collaboration. Unpublished dissertation, The University of Adelaide.

Craven, David/Morelli, Nicola (2004): Logical Spaces for Urban Nomads. Royal Melbourne Institute of Technology.

Creischer, Alice/Hinderer, Max Jorge/ Siekmann, Andreas (eds.) (2010): The Potosí Principle. How Can We Sing the Song of the Lord in an Alien Land? Cologne: Walther König.

Danwei (2005): China Media Guide. 07.08.2005 http://www.danwei.org/editorial/china_media_guide.php [accessed 08 September 2011]

Davis, Deborah (1995): Urban spaces in contemporary China. Washington, D.C.: Woodrow Wilson Center Press; Cambridge: Cambridge University Press.

Deleuze, Gilles/Félix Guattari. (2004 [1987]): A thousand plateaus: capitalism and schizophrenia. London: Continuum.

DESA (2011): United Nations. Department of Economic and Social Affairs (2011): Population Division. www.un.org/esa/population [accessed 09 July 2011]

DRC (2011): Development Research Centre on Migration, Globalisation & Poverty. http://www.migrationdrc.org/ [accessed 09 July 2011]

DVP (2011): Deutscher Verband der Projektmanager in der Bau- und Immobilienwirtschaft. http://www.dvpev.de [accessed 01 May 2011]

EPCM (2011): Engineering, Procurement and Construction Management. www.epcengineer.com [accessed 25 September 2011]

EU SME (2015): Sector Report: The Construction Sector in China. www.ccilic.pt/sites/default/files/eu_sme_centre_repor_the_construction_sector_in_china_update_-_june_2015.pdf. [accessed 25 January 2016]

Fair Trade Foundation (2011): http://www.fairtrade.org.uk [accessed 26 May 2011]

Fan, Cindy (2008): China on the move. Migration, the state, and the household. London and New York: Routledge.

Friedmann, John (2005): China's urban transition. Minneapolis: University of Minnesota Press.

Fulong, Wu in Xiangming Chen (ed.) (2006) Local Transformations in Global Cities: Shanghai in Comparative Perspective. Minneapolis: University of Minnesota Press: http://www.cardiff.ac.uk/cplan/resources/Globalizationthe ChangingStateandLocalGovernanceinShanghai.pdf [accessed 25 September 2011]

Gaubatz, Piper (2008): New Public Space in Urban China. Fewer Walls, More Malls in Beijing, Shangai and Xining. China Perspectives N°2008/4, Hong Kong: Hop Sze Printing.

GB/T 50378 (2006): Standard by People's Republic of China Evaluation Standard for Green Buildings. http://neec.no/uploads/Evaluation%20standard%20 for%20green%20buildings.pdf [accessed December 2015]

GBL (2009): Green Building Label China, Evaluation Standard for Green Building). Chinagreenbuildings.blogspot.co.at/2009/2´02/ministry-of-construction -green-building.html [accessed 26 September 2011]

Gensler (2011): Design Update Shanghai Tower. http://www.gensler.com/ uploads/documents/Shanghai_Tower_12_22_2010.pdf [accessed 19 September 2011]

Gil, Iker (eds.) (2008): Shanghai transforming: The changing physical, economic, social, and environmental conditions of a global metropolis (1st ed.). Barcelona: Actar.

Goethe Institute Shanghai (2011): http://www.goethe.de/ins/cn/sha/deindex.htm [accessed 25 September 2011]

Graham, Stephen/Healey, Patsy (1999): Relational concepts for space and place: Issues for planning theory and practice, European Studies Planning Studies Volume 7, Issue 5, 1999, p.623-646

Gugler, Josef (eds.) (2004): World cities beyond the West: globalization, development, and Inequality. Cambridge: Cambridge University Press.

Hassenpflug, Dieter (2010): The Urban Code of China. Basel: Birkhäuser Verlag.

HOAI (2011): http://www.hoai.de [accessed 27 April 2011]

Hofstede, Geert (2001[1983]): Culture's Consequences: Comparing Values, Behaviors, Institutions and Organizations Across Nations.Thousand Oaks, London: Sage Publications Inc, 2nd edition.

Hsing, You-Tian (2010): The Great Urban Transformation. Politics of Land and Property in China. New York: Oxford University Press.

Huang, Yedan (2008): Return migration. A case study of "sea turtles" in Shanghai. Unpublished Masterthesis. The University of Hong Kong.

Human Development Report China 2007/08 (2008). Access for all: Basic public services for 1.3 billion people. Beijing: China Translation and Publishing Corporation.

Human Rights Watch (2008): One Year of My Blood. Volume 20, No. 3(C). http://www.hrw.org/sites/default/files/reports/china0308webwcover.pdf [accessed September 2011]

IHLO (2011): Hong Kong Liaison Office of the International Trade Union Movement, http://www.ihlo.org/index.html, [accessed 27 September 2011]

ILO (2011): International Labour Organization: Mission and objectives. http://www.ilo.org/global/about-the-ilo/mission-and-objectives/lang--en/index.htm [accessed 19 October 2011]

IOM (2010): International Organization for Migration. World migration report 2010: The future of migration : building capacities for change. World migration report. Geneva: International Organization for Migration.

IMF (2015): Understanding Residential Real Estate in China. IMF Workding Paper. https://www.imf.org/external/pubs/ft/wp/2015/wp1584.pdf [accessed 19 December 2015]

Jacka, Tamara (2005): Rural women in urban China. Gender, migration, and social change. Armonk, N.Y.: M.E. Sharpe, Inc.

Johnston, Tess (2010): Permanentley Temporary. From Berlin to Shanghai in Half a Century. Old China Hand Press.

Keith, Michael (2011): Citizenship in Contemporary China: Shanghai, Capital of the Twenty-First Century. In Bridge, G. and Watson, S. (eds.): The New Blackwell Companion to the City. West Sussex, UK: Blackwell Publishing, , pp. 398-406.

Knierbein, Sabine (2010): Die Produktion zentraler öffentlicher Räume in der Aufmerksamkeitsökonomie. Ästhetische, ökonomische und mediale Restrukturierungen durch gestaltwirksame Koalitionen in Berlin seit 1980 (1.ed.). Wiesbaden: VS Verlag für Sozialwissenschaften.

Kochendörfer, Bernd/Liebchen, Jens/ Viering, Markus (2008): Bau-Projekt-Management: Grundlagen und Vorgehensweisen (4., aktualis. u. erw. Aufl.). Leitfaden des Baubetriebs und der Bauwirtschaft. Wiesbaden: Vieweg + Teubner in GWV Fachverlage GmbH.

Koolhaas, Rem (2004): Content. Triumph of Relization. Köln: Taschen Verlag.

Krüger, Justus (2010): Gute Aussicht auf Besserung. Enorm, No. 4, Hamburg: Social Publish Verlag GmbH, p.94.

LAC (2011): Labour Action China labour rights nongovernmental organization, http://www.lac.org.hk/en/, [accessed 28 September 2011]

Ladewig, Rebekka/Mellinger, Nan (2003): When in doubt: go nomad. Zur Gegenwart des Nomadischen. In: Alexander Meschnig und Matthias Stuhr (eds.) Arbeit als Lebensstil. Frankfurt am Main: Suhrkamp. p.44-56

Leach, Neil (2001): The Aesthetic Cocoon. In OASE, 54, Winter 2001, pp. 1004-121. https://neilleach.files.wordpress.com/2009/09/aesthetic-cocoon.pdf [accessed 28 September 2011]

Lee Ching Kwan (2011): Sociology 185 - Lecture 6: GLOBAL SOCIOLOGY: Ching Kwan Lee on the Enigma of Chinese, March 2011. [video online] http://www.youtube.com/watch?v=XXyCAYv33Gk

LEED (2011): Leadership in Energy and Environmental Design, http://www.leed.net/, http://www.worldgbc.org/site2/ [accessed 24 September 2011]

Lefebvre, Henri (2003 [1970]): The Urban Revolution. (translated into English by Robert Bononno) Minneapolis: The University Press of Minnesota.

Lefebvre, Henri (2009 [1974]): The production of space. (translated into English by Donald Nicholson-Smith) Malden: Blackwell Publishing.

Li, Cao (2016): China Moves to Halt 'Weird' Architecture. In The New York Times 22.02.2016. http://mobile.nytimes.com/2016/02/23/world/asia/china-weird architecture.html?_r=4&referer=http://www.archdaily.com/782661/china-takes-steps-to-stop-its-weird-architecture [accessed 16 February 2016]

Li, Xiangning/Zhang, Xiachun (2008): Dreaming of Collective Dwelling in Shanghai: From Lilong to International Community in Gil, Iker: Shanghai Transforming. Barcelona: Actar.

Li, Yuwen (2011): NGOs in China and Europe: Comparisons and contrasts. Farnham: Ashgate.

Lifecyle Building Challenge (2011): http://www.lifecyclebuilding.org [access 13 July 2011]

Logan, John R. (2002): The new Chinese city. Globalization and market reform. Oxford: Blackwell Publishers.

Lu, Xin (2008): China, China... Western Architects and City Planners in China. China: Hatje Cantz Verlag.

Luft, Stefan/Schimany, Peter (eds.) (2010): Integration von Zuwanderern. Erfahrungen, Konzepte, Perspektiven. Bielefeld: transcript Verlag.

Ma, Laurence J.C./Wu Fulong (2005): Restructuring the Chinese city: Changing society, economy and space. London: Routledge.

Macauley, David (2002): Walking the City: an Essay on Peripatetic Practices and Politics. In Backhaus, Gary/ Murungi, John (eds): Transformations of urban and suburban landscapes. Perspectives from Philosophy, Geography, and Architecture. Maryland and Oxford: Lexington Books.

Madanipour, Ali (2003): Public and Private Spaces of the City. London: Routledge.

McMillan, John/Naughton, Barry (1996): Reforming Asian socialism: The growth of market institutions. Ann Arbor: University of Michigan Press.

McKinsey Global Institue (2009): Preparing for China's urban billion (February 2009) http://www.mckinsey.com/insights/urbanization/preparing_for_urban_billion_in_china [accessed 04 July 2011]

Mercer (2014): Global Moblity: Moving the Right People tot he Right Place at the Right Cost. www.imercer.com [accessed 15 January 2016]

Milgrom, Richard/Lucien Kroll (2008): Design, difference, everyday life. In Goonewardena, Kanishka; Kipfer, Stefan; Milgrom, Richard; Schmid, Christian (eds): Space, Difference, Everyday Life. Reading Henri Lefebvre. London and New York: Routledge.

Miller, Tom (2012): China's urban billion: The story behind the biggest migration in human history. Asian arguments. London: Zed.

Minter, Adam (2010): Disappearing Shanghai: The Roots of an Urban Tragedy, Pt.I. 11.08.2010 http://shanghaiscrap.com/2010/08/disappearing-shanghai-roots-of-an-urban-tragedy-pt-1/ [accessed 30 September 2011]

Murphy, Rachel (2009): Labour Migration and Social Development in Contemporary China. London & New York: Routledge.

Muynck (2009): Architecture practice in China. http://www.culturalexchange-cn.nl/mapping-china/architecture/architecture-practice-china [accessed 19 September 2011]

Na Li (2007): China Watch: Foreign Architecture Firms Doing Design Activities in China. http://www.thelenreid.com/index.cfm?section=articles&function=ViewArticle&articleID=3248 [accessed 19 September 2011]

Naughton, Barry (1995): Growing Out of the Plan: Chinese Economic Reform, 1978-1993. Cambridge: Cambridge University Press.

National Bureau of Statistics of China – NBSC (2011): China Statistical Yearbook 2009. http://www.stats.gov.cn/tjsj/ndsj/2009/indexeh.htm [accessed 21 April 2011]

National Bureau of Statistics of China.– NBSC (2014):China Statistical Yearbook 2014. http://www.stats.gov.cn/tjsj/ndsj/2014/indexeh.htm. [accessed 30 December 2015]

Nielsen, Ingrid (2008): Migration and social protection in China. Hackensack, NJ: World Scientific.

Norberg-Schulz, Christian (1980): Genius Loci- Towards a phenomenology of Architecture. Chapter: The Phenomenon of Place. New York: Rizzoli.

Pattisson, Pete (2013): Revealed: Qatar's World Cup 'slaves': Exclusive: Abuse and exploitation of migrant workers preparing emirate for 2022. The Guardian, 25.09.2013. Retrieved from http://www.theguardian.com/world/2013/sep/25/revealed-qatars-world-cup-slaves, last accessed on 28.04.2014

Pels, Dick (1999): Priviledged Nomads. On the Strangeness of Intellectuals and the Intellectuality of Strangers. In Theory, Culture & Society. Vol. 16(1), London: SAGE and New Delhi: Thousand Oaks.

PMI (2011): Project Management Institute. http://www.pmi.org/ [accessed 12 May 2011]

Pun, Ngai/ Lee, Ching Kwan (2010): Aufbruch der zweiten Generation. Wanderarbeit, Gender und Klassenzusammensetzung in China. Berlin/Hamburg: Assoziation.

Pun, Ngai/Xu, Yi (2011): Legal Activism or Class Action? The political economy of the "no boss" and "no labour relationship in China's construction industry". China Perspectives, No 2011/2. Pp. 9-17.

RAS (2011): Royal Asiatic Society China in Shanghai. http://www.royal asiaticsociety.org.cn/0801/0803/Events.html [accessed 25 September 2011]

ren ren (2014). Chinese social network. http://www.renren.com/ [accessed 03 October 2014]

Research School of Economics (2010): Rural-Urban Migration in China and Indonesia (RUMiCI). 4/2010 http://rumici.anu.edu.au/joomla/index.php?option =com_content&task=view&id=49&Itemid=52 [accessed 10 April 2011]

RIBA (2013): RIBA. Plan of Work 2013. http://www.ribaplanofwork.com/about/Concept.aspx. [accessed 03 January 2015]

Rutten, Koen (2010): Confucian Capitalism: An inquiry into the relationship between East Asian Thought and Firm Performance, unpublished Masterthesis; Erasmus University Rotterdam.

Sassen, Saskia (2001): The global city. New York, London, Tokyo. Princeton, New Jersey: Princeton University Press 2d ed.

Saunders, Doug (2011): Arrival city. London: Windmill Books.

Schanghai.com. deutschsprachige China-Plattform. http://www.schanghai.com/ [accessed 25 September 2011]

Schaub, Christoph/Schindhelm, Michael (2008): The Bird's Nest. Herzog & de Meuron in China, 2008. [movie] http://www.herzogdemeuron-film.com/

Schauhuber, Stefan (2010): Interne Migration und Entwicklung: Die Regulation der Binnenmigration als Bestandteil der chinesischen Entwicklungsstrategie. Unpublished Masterthesis at University of Vienna.

Schein, Louisa (2006): Urbanity, Cosmopolitanism, Consumption. In Chen/Clark (eds.) (2006): China Urban. Ethnographies of Contemporary Culture. Durham&London: Duke University Press.

Scott, James C. (1998): Seeing Like a State. The High-Modernist City: An Experiment and a Critique. Yale University Press.

SEA (2011): Shanghai Expatriate Association. http://www.seashanghai.org/ [accessed 25 September 2011]

Sennett, Richard (2008): The craftsman. New Haven: Yale University Press

Shanghai Government Legislative Information Network (2010): Notice of Shanghai Municipal People's Government on Approving and Transmitting the Shanghai's Standards of Eligibility for Provision of Affordable Housing (2010). 07.08.2010. http://www.shanghailaw.gov.cn/fzbEnglish/page/normative14642.htm [accessed 14 June 2011]

Shanghai Statistical (2014): Shanghai Municipal Government. http://www.stats-sh.gov.cn/tjnj/zgsh/nj2011.html. [accessed 30 December 2015]

Shi, Li (2010): The Economic Situation of Rural Migrant Workers in China. In China Perspectives N. 2010/4, Hong Kong: Hop Sze Printing.

Shieh, Shawn (2015): Non-governmental organisations. Uncivil society. A new draft law spooks foreign not-for-profit groups working in China. http://www.economist.com/news/china/21661819-new-draft-law-spooks-foreign-not-profit-groups-working-china-uncivil-society [accessed 10 January 2016]

Shields, Rob (1999): Lefebvre, Love & Struggle. Spatial Dialectics. New York: Routledge.

Sinclair, Cameron (2007): Design Like You Give a Damn. Architectural responses to humanitarian crisis. London: Thames&Hudson.

Sommers, Amy/Phillips, Kara (2010): A Tragedy of Commons: Property Rights Issues in Shanghai Historic Residences. Penn State International Law Review Vol. 28, Seattle University School of Law Research Paper No. 10:06.

Stepping Stones (2011): NGO - Shanghai Volunteer English Teaching Program. http://steppingstoneschina.net [accessed 21 April 2011]

Stiglechner, Leonore (2009): Volunteer Tourismus. Eine anthropologische Analyse. Unpublished Masterthesis. Universität Wien.

Sun, Heng (2011): Culture and Arts Museum of Migrant Labourers. http://www.dagongwenhua.org.cn/ [accessed 27 September 2011]

Tay, Sue Anne (2011): The face of Shanghai's skyline. In Shanghai Street Stories. www.shanghaistreetstories.com [accessed 08 August 2011]

The Oxford Dictionary (2011). www.oxforddictionaries.com, [accessed 13 July 2011]

Tornaghi, Chiara (2009): Challenges. Planungskulturen und sensible gesellschaftliche Sphären. TU Wien.
Trading Economics (2007): International migrant stock. www.tradingeconomics.com [accessed 08 September 2011]
UN Habitat (1996): The Recife Declaration 1996 Recife International Meeting on Urban Poverty, Recife, Brazil, 17-21 March 1996. http://ww2.unhabitat.org/programmes/ifup/rde.asp [accessed 28 September 2011]
UN General Assembly (1990): International Convention on the Protection of the Rights of All Migrant Workers and Members of their Families, 18 December 1990, A/RES/45/158, http://www.refworld.org/docid/3ae6b3980.html [accessed 1 February 2016]
United Nations/UN (2004): World Population to 2300 report. New York. http://www.un.org/esa/population/publications/longrange2/WorldPop2300final.pdf [accessed 21 April 2011]
United Nations Development Programme/UNDP (2009): Human Development Reports. http://hdr.undp.org/en/media/HDR_2009_EN_Complete.pdf [accessed 30 September 2011]
Wang, Xiaoming (2011): The City's New "Trinity" in Contemporary Shanghai: A Case Study of the Residential Housing Market. In Bridge, Gary and Waston, Sophie (eds): The New Blackwell Companion to the City. West Sussex, UK: Blackwell Publishing.
Wang, Ya Ping/Wan, Yanglin (2009): Labour Migration and Social Development in Contemporary China. Housing and Migrants in Cities. London and New York: Routledge.
Wang, Ya Ping/Wan, Yanglin/Wu, Jiansheng (2007): Housing Conditions of Migrant Workers in Shenzhen. College of Environmental Sciences of Beijing University.
Wei Wei (2011): Little Bird. http://www.xiaoxiaoniao.org.cn/ [accessed on 27 September 2011]
Wemheuer, Felix (2011): "Die zweite Generation: Wanderarbeiter in China", 150207 MA-PS GG. Unpublished Paper. University of Vienna.
Wiegand, Dietmar (2008): Mini Skriptum zu den Grundbegriffen der Projektentwicklung. Unpublished Paper. Technische Universität Wien.
Wing, Chang Kam /Buckingham, Will (2008): Is China Abolishing the Hukou System? in The China Quarterly, Ort: Cambridge University Press.
Winkler, Roland (2011): Sustainable Architecture. German Innovations Enable a Low-Carbon Future. Free Bi-Monthly Newsletter of the German Chamber of Commerce in China- Issue 3.

World Bank (2015): Urban population (% of total). http://data.worldbank.org/indicator/SP.URB.TOTL.IN.ZS [accessed on 27 January 2016]

Wrightsman, Bruce (2007): Urban Nomad. In Eindhoven: Tectonics Making Meaning. International Conference Einhoven. University of Technology.

Wu, Fulong (2005): Rediscovering the "Gate" Under Market Transition: From Work-unit Compounds to Commodity Housing Enclaves. Housing Studies, Vol. 20, No. 2, March, 2005, p.235-254.

Wu, Fulong/Webber, Klaire (2004): The rise of "foreign gated communities" in Beijing: between economic globalization and local institutions. Department of Geography, University of Southampton.

Wu, Fulong/Xu, Jiang/Yeh, Anthony Gar-On (2007): Urban development in post-reform China. State, Market and Space. London: Routledge.

Xue, Charlie Q.L./Zhou, Minghao (2007): Importation and adaptation: building 'one city and nine towns' in Shanghai: a case study of Vittorio Gregotti's pland of Pujiang Town. Urban Design International, 12(1), 21–40.

Yan, Hairong (2008): New Masters, New Servants. Migration, Development, and Women Workers in China. Durham and London: Duke University Press.

Zai, Liang (2006): The Age of Migration in China. Population and Development Review. Vol. 27, No. 3 (Sep., 2001), pp. 499-524.

Zakaria, Fareed (2010): The New Challenge From China. Time Magazine Asia: Wen's World. Issue Vol. 176, No. 16; October 18th, 2010, p. 30 – 33.

Zhou, Shaoqing (2011): A review of the development of Labour Organization in China in the 30 Years Since the reform and Opening up. In Li, Yuwen (eds.) (2011): NGOs in China and Europe: Comparisons and Contrasts. Farnham and Burlington: Ashgate Publishing Limited.

Zhu, Jianfei (2005): Criticality in between China and the West. The Journal of Architecture. 10(5). Chicago: Paper.

Zhu, Jieming (2000): The Changing Mode of Housing Provision in Transitional China. Urban Affairs Review, 35(4), SAGE Publications.

Table of Figures

The pictures and figures in this book are taken and created by Ulrike Bronner and Clarissa Reikersdorfer

Box 1 – Three Components of the Social Production of Space
Box 2 – The Vision of China's Urbanization in 2025
Box 3 – People in Motion
Box 4 – Migration

Figure 1 – Laundry Hanging in a Half Demolished House in Shanghai
Figure 2 – Builders of Shanghai's Skyline
Figure 3 – Shanghai Street Life
Figure 4 – Three Components of the Social Production of Space
Figure 5 – Construction Site in Kunshan/Shanghai
Figure 6 – Key Stages of the Construction Process
Figure 7 – Stakeholders. Who is Involved?
Figure 8 – Internal Migration in China
Figure 9 – International Migration to China
Figure 10 – Societies Influenced by Migration
Figure 11 – Large Scale – Urban Scale – The Excluded User
Figure 12 – Medium Scale – Living Environment – The Excluded Consumer
Figure 13 – Small Scale – Building Projects – Intersections Between the Involved
Figure 14 – Analytical Frame – Production of Space
Figure 15 – Shanghai, View on Pudong
Figure 16 – m² Floor Area in Shanghai by Year
Figure 17 – Resident Foreigners in Shanghai by Types
Figure 18 – The Number of Rural Migrant Workers in Various Years
Figure 19 – Subcontracting System on a Chinese Construction Site